Sesame and Lilies

John Ruskin

ESPRIOS DIGITAL PUBLISHING

CONTENTS

LECTURE I—SESAME. OF KING'S TREASURIES

"You shall each have a cake of sesame, —and ten pound. " Lucian: The Fisherman.

My first duty this evening is to ask your pardon for the ambiguity of title under which the subject of lecture has been announced: for indeed I am not going to talk of kings, known as regnant, nor of treasuries, understood to contain wealth; but of quite another order of royalty, and another material of riches, than those usually acknowledged. I had even intended to ask your attention for a little while on trust, and (as sometimes one contrives, in taking a friend to see a favourite piece of scenery) to hide what I wanted most to show, with such imperfect cunning as I might, until we unexpectedly reached the best point of view by winding paths. But— and as also I have heard it said, by men practised in public address, that hearers are never so much fatigued as by the endeavour to follow a speaker who gives them no clue to his purpose, —I will take the slight mask off at once, and tell you plainly that I want to speak to you about the treasures hidden in books; and about the way we find them, and the way we lose them. A grave subject, you will say; and a wide one! Yes; so wide that I shall make no effort to touch the compass of it. I will try only to bring before you a few simple thoughts about reading, which press themselves upon me every day more deeply, as I watch the course of the public mind with respect to our daily enlarging means of education; and the answeringly wider spreading on the levels, of the irrigation of literature.

It happens that I have practically some connexion with schools for different classes of youth; and I receive many letters from parents respecting the education of their children. In the mass of these letters I am always struck by the precedence which the idea of a "position in life" takes above all other thoughts in the parents'— more especially in the mothers'—minds. "The education befitting such and such a STATION IN LIFE"—this is the phrase, this the object, always. They never seek, as far as I can make out, an education good in itself; even the conception of abstract rightness in training rarely seems reached by the writers. But, an education "which shall keep a good coat on my son's back; —which shall enable him to ring with confidence the visitors' bell at double-belled doors; which shall result ultimately in establishment of a double- belled door to his own house; —in a word, which shall lead to advancement in life; —THIS we pray for on bent knees—and this is ALL we pray for. " It never seems to occur to the parents that there may be an education which, in itself, IS advancement in Life; —that any other than that may perhaps be advancement in Death; and that this essential education might be more easily got, or given, than they fancy, if they set about it in the right way; while it is for no price, and by no favour, to be got, if they set about it in the wrong.

Indeed, among the ideas most prevalent and effective in the mind of this busiest of countries, I suppose the first—at least that which is confessed with the greatest frankness, and put forward as the fittest stimulus to youthful exertion—is this of "Advancement in life. " May I ask you to consider with me, what this idea practically includes, and what it should include?

Practically, then, at present, "advancement in life" means, becoming conspicuous in life; obtaining a position which shall be acknowledged by others to be respectable or honourable. We do not understand by this advancement, in general, the mere making of money, but the being known to have made it; not the accomplishment of any great aim, but the being seen to have accomplished it. In a word, we mean the gratification of our thirst for applause. That thirst, if the last infirmity of noble minds, is also the first infirmity of weak ones; and, on the whole, the strongest impulsive influence of average humanity: the greatest efforts of the race have always been traceable to the love of praise, as its greatest catastrophes to the love of pleasure.

I am not about to attack or defend this impulse. I want you only to feel how it lies at the root of effort; especially of all modern effort. It is the gratification of vanity which is, with us, the stimulus of toil and balm of repose; so closely does it touch the very springs of life that the wounding of our vanity is always spoken of (and truly) as in its measure MORTAL; we call it "mortification, " using the same expression which we should apply to a gangrenous and incurable bodily hurt. And although a few of us may be physicians enough to recognise the various effect of this passion upon health and energy, I believe most honest men know, and would at once acknowledge, its leading power with them as a motive. The seaman does not commonly desire to be made captain only because he knows he can manage the ship better than any other sailor on board. He wants to be made captain that he may be CALLED captain. The clergyman does not usually want to be made a bishop only because he believes that no other hand can, as firmly as his, direct the diocese through its difficulties. He wants to be made bishop primarily that he may be called "My Lord. " And a prince does not usually desire to enlarge, or a subject to gain, a kingdom, because he believes no one else can as well serve the State, upon its throne; but, briefly, because he wishes to be addressed as "Your Majesty, " by as many lips as may be brought to such utterance.

This, then, being the main idea of "advancement in life, " the force of it applies, for all of us, according to our station, particularly to that secondary result of such advancement which we call "getting into good society. " We want to get into good society, not that we may have it, but that we may be seen in it; and our notion of its goodness depends primarily on its conspicuousness.

Will you pardon me if I pause for a moment to put what I fear you may think an impertinent question? I never can go on with an address unless I feel, or know, that my audience are either with me or against me: I do not much care which, in beginning; but I must know where they are; and I would fain find out, at this instant, whether you think I am putting the motives of popular action too low. I am resolved, to-night, to state them low enough to be admitted as probable; for whenever, in my writings on Political Economy, I assume that a little honesty, or generosity, —or what used to be called "virtue, "—may be calculated upon as a human motive of action, people always answer me, saying, "You must not calculate on that: that is not in human nature: you must not assume anything to be common to men but acquisitiveness and jealousy; no other feeling ever has influence on them, except accidentally, and in matters out of the way of business. " I begin, accordingly, tonight low in the scale of motives; but I must know if you think me right in doing so. Therefore, let me ask those who admit the love of praise to be usually the strongest motive in men's minds in seeking advancement, and the honest desire of doing any kind of duty to be an entirely secondary one, to hold up their hands. (About a dozen hands held up—the audience, partly, not being sure the lecturer is serious, and, partly, shy of expressing opinion.) I am quite serious—I really do want to know what you think; however, I can judge by putting the reverse question. Will those who think that duty is generally the first, and love of praise the second, motive, hold up their hands? (One hand reported to have been held up behind the lecturer.) Very good: I see you are with me, and that you think I have not begun too near the ground. Now, without teasing you by putting farther question, I venture to assume that you will admit duty as at least a secondary or tertiary motive. You think that the desire of doing something useful, or obtaining some real good, is indeed an existent collateral idea, though a secondary one, in most men's desire of advancement. You will grant that moderately honest men desire place and office, at least in some measure for the sake of beneficent power; and would wish to associate rather with sensible and well-informed persons than with fools and ignorant persons, whether they are seen in the company of the sensible ones or not. And finally, without being troubled by repetition of any common truisms about the preciousness of friends, and the influence of companions, you will admit, doubtless, that according to the sincerity of our desire that our friends may be true, and our companions wise, —and in proportion to the earnestness and discretion with which we choose both, —will be the general chances of our happiness and usefulness.

But, granting that we had both the will and the sense to choose our friends well, how few of us have the power! or, at least, how limited, for most, is the sphere of choice! Nearly all our associations are determined by chance or necessity; and restricted within a narrow circle. We cannot know whom we would; and those whom we know, we cannot have at our side when we most need them. All the higher circles of human intelligence are, to those beneath, only momentarily and partially open. We may, by good fortune, obtain a glimpse of a great poet, and hear the sound of his voice; or put a question to a man of science, and be answered good- humouredly. We may intrude ten minutes' talk on a cabinet minister, answered probably with words worse than silence, being deceptive; or snatch, once or twice in our lives, the privilege of throwing a bouquet in the path of a princess, or arresting the kind glance of a queen. And yet these momentary chances we covet; and spend our years, and passions, and powers, in pursuit of little more than these; while, meantime, there is a society continually open to us, of people who will talk to us as long as we like, whatever our rank or occupation; —talk to us in the best words they can choose, and of the things nearest their hearts. And this society, because it is so numerous and so gentle, and can be kept waiting round us all day long, —kings and statesmen lingering patiently, not to grant audience, but to gain it! —in those plainly furnished and narrow ante-rooms, our bookcase shelves, —we make no account of that company, —perhaps never listen to a word they would say, all day long!

You may tell me, perhaps, or think within yourselves, that the apathy with which we regard this company of the noble, who are praying us to listen to them; and the passion with which we pursue the company, probably of the ignoble, who despise us, or who have nothing to teach us, are grounded in this, —that we can see the faces of the living men, and it is themselves, and not their sayings, with which we desire to become familiar. But it is not so. Suppose you never were to see their faces; —suppose you could be put behind a screen in the statesman's cabinet, or the prince's chamber, would you not be glad to listen to their words, though you were forbidden to advance beyond the screen? And when the screen is only a little less, folded in two instead of four, and you can be hidden behind the cover of the two boards that bind a book, and listen all day long, not to the casual talk, but to the studied, determined, chosen addresses of the wisest of men; —this station of audience, and honourable privy council, you despise!

But perhaps you will say that it is because the living people talk of things that are passing, and are of immediate interest to you, that you desire to hear them. Nay; that cannot be so, for the living people will themselves tell you about passing matters much better in their writings than in their careless talk. Yet I admit that this motive does influence you, so far as you prefer those rapid and ephemeral writings to slow and enduring writings—books, properly so called. For all books are divisible into two classes, the books of the hour, and the books of all time. Mark this distinction—it is not one of quality only. It is not merely the bad book that does not last, and the good one that does. It is a distinction of species. There are good books for the hour, and good ones for all time; bad books for the hour, and bad ones for all time. I must define the two kinds before I go farther.

The good book of the hour, then, —I do not speak of the bad ones, —is simply the useful or pleasant talk of some person whom you cannot otherwise converse with, printed for you. Very useful often, telling you what you need to know; very pleasant often, as a sensible friend's present talk would be. These bright accounts of travels; good-humoured and witty discussions of question; lively or pathetic story-telling in the form of novel; firm fact-telling, by the real agents concerned in the events of passing history; —all these books of the hour, multiplying among us as education becomes more general, are a peculiar possession of the present age: we ought to be entirely thankful for them, and entirely ashamed of ourselves if we make no good use of them. But we make the worst possible use if we allow them to usurp the place of true books: for, strictly speaking, they are not books at all, but merely letters or newspapers in good print. Our friend's letter may be delightful, or necessary, to-day: whether worth keeping or not, is to be considered. The newspaper may be entirely proper at breakfast time, but assuredly it is not reading for all day. So, though bound up in a volume, the long letter which gives you so pleasant an account of the inns, and roads, and weather, last year at such a place, or which tells you that amusing story, or gives you the real circumstances of such and such events, however valuable for occasional reference, may not be, in the real sense of the word, a "book" at all, nor, in the real sense, to be "read. " A book is essentially not a talking thing, but a written thing; and written, not with a view of mere communication, but of permanence. The book of talk is printed only because its author cannot speak to thousands of people at once; if he could, he would—the volume is mere MULTIPLICATION of his voice. You cannot talk to your friend in India; if you could, you would; you write instead: that is mere CONVEYANCE of voice. But a book is written, not to multiply the voice merely, not to carry it merely, but to perpetuate it. The author has something to say which he perceives to be true and useful, or helpfully beautiful. So far as he knows, no one has yet said it; so far as he knows, no one else can say it. He is bound to say it, clearly and melodiously if he may; clearly at all events. In the sum of his life he finds this to be the thing, or group of things, manifest to him; —this, the piece of true knowledge, or sight, which his share of sunshine and earth has permitted him to seize. He would fain set it down for ever; engrave it on rock, if he could; saying, "This is the best of me; for the rest, I ate, and drank, and slept, loved, and hated, like another; my life was as the vapour, and is not; but this I saw and knew: this, if anything of mine, is worth your memory. " That is his "writing; " it is, in his small human way, and with whatever degree of true inspiration is in him, his inscription, or scripture. That is a "Book. "

Perhaps you think no books were ever so written?

But, again, I ask you, do you at all believe in honesty, or at all in kindness, or do you think there is never any honesty or benevolence in wise people? None of us, I hope, are so unhappy as to think that. Well, whatever bit of a wise man's work is honestly and benevolently done, that bit is his book or his piece of art. {5} It is mixed always with evil fragments—ill-done, redundant, affected work. But if you read rightly, you will easily discover the true bits, and those ARE the book.

Now books of this kind have been written in all ages by their greatest men: - by great readers, great statesmen, and great thinkers. These are all at your choice; and Life is short. You have heard as much before; —yet have you measured and mapped out this short life and its possibilities? Do you know, if you read this, that you cannot read that—that what you lose to-day you cannot gain to-morrow? Will you go and gossip with your housemaid, or your stable-boy, when you may talk with queens and kings; or flatter yourself that it is with any worthy consciousness of your own claims to respect, that you jostle with the hungry and common crowd for ENTREE here, and audience there, when all the while this eternal court is open to you, with its society, wide as the world, multitudinous as its days, the chosen, and the mighty, of every place and time? Into that you may enter always; in that you may take fellowship and rank according to your wish; from that, once entered into it, you can never be outcast but by your own fault; by your aristocracy of companionship there, your own inherent aristocracy will be assuredly tested, and the motives with which you strive to take high place in the society of the living, measured, as to all the truth and sincerity that are in them, by the place you desire to take in this company of the Dead.

"The place you desire, " and the place you FIT YOURSELF FOR, I must also say; because, observe, this court of the past differs from all living aristocracy in this: - it is open to labour and to merit, but to nothing else. No wealth will bribe, no name overawe, no artifice deceive, the guardian of those Elysian gates. In the deep sense, no vile or vulgar person ever enters there. At the portieres of that silent Faubourg St. Germain, there is but brief question: - "Do you deserve to enter? Pass. Do you ask to be the companion of nobles? Make yourself noble, and you shall be. Do you long for the conversation of the wise? Learn to understand it, and you shall hear it. But on other terms? —no. If you will not rise to us, we cannot stoop to you. The living lord may assume courtesy, the living philosopher explain his thought to you with considerate pain; but here we neither feign nor interpret; you must rise to the level of our thoughts if you would be gladdened by them, and share our feelings, if you would recognise our presence. "

This, then, is what you have to do, and I admit that it is much. You must, in a word, love these people, if you are to be among them. No ambition is of any use. They scorn your ambition. You must love them, and show your love in these two following ways.

(1) First, by a true desire to be taught by them, and to enter into their thoughts. To enter into theirs, observe; not to find your own expressed by them. If the person who wrote the book is not wiser than you, you need not read it; if he be, he will think differently from you in many respects.

(2) Very ready we are to say of a book, "How good this is—that's exactly what I think! " But the right feeling is, "How strange that is! I never thought of that before, and yet I see it is true; or if I do not now, I hope I shall, some day. " But whether thus submissively or not, at least be sure that you go to the author to get at HIS meaning, not to find yours. Judge it afterwards if you think yourself qualified to do so; but ascertain it first. And be sure, also, if the author is worth anything, that you will not get at his meaning all at once; —nay, that at his whole meaning you will not for a long time arrive in any wise. Not that he does not say what he means, and in strong words too; but he cannot say it all; and what is more strange, will not, but in a hidden way and in parables, in order that he may be sure you want it. I cannot quite see the reason of this, nor analyse that cruel reticence in the breasts of wise men which makes them always hide their deeper thought. They do not give it you by way of help, but of reward; and will make themselves sure that you deserve it before they allow you to reach it. But it is the same with the physical type of wisdom, gold. There seems, to you and me, no reason why the electric forces of the earth should not carry whatever there is of gold within it at once to the mountain tops, so that kings and people might know that all the gold they could get was there; and without any trouble of digging, or anxiety, or chance, or waste of time, cut it away, and coin as much as they needed. But Nature does not manage it so. She puts it in little fissures in the earth, nobody knows where: you may dig long and find none; you must dig painfully to find any.

And it is just the same with men's best wisdom. When you come to a good book, you must ask yourself, "Am I inclined to work as an Australian miner would? Are my pickaxes and shovels in good order, and am I in good trim myself, my sleeves well up to the elbow, and my breath good, and my temper? " And, keeping the figure a little longer, even at cost of tiresomeness, for it is a thoroughly useful one, the metal you are in search of being the author's mind or meaning, his words are as the rock which you have to crush and smelt in order to get at it. And your pickaxes are your own care, wit, and learning; your smelting furnace is your own thoughtful soul. Do not hope to get at any good author's meaning without those tools and that fire; often you will need sharpest, finest chiselling, and patientest fusing, before you can gather one grain of the metal.

And, therefore, first of all, I tell you earnestly and authoritatively (I KNOW I am right in this), you must get into the habit of looking intensely at words, and assuring yourself of their meaning, syllable by syllable—nay, letter by letter. For though it is only by reason of the opposition of letters in the function of signs, to sounds in the function of signs, that the study of books is called "literature, " and that a man versed in it is called, by the consent of nations, a man of letters instead of a man of books, or of words, you may yet connect with that accidental nomenclature this real fact: - that you might read all the books in the British Museum (if you could live long enough), and remain an utterly "illiterate, " uneducated person; but that if you read ten pages of a good book, letter by letter, —that is to say, with real accuracy, — you are for evermore in some measure an educated person. The entire difference between education and non-education (as regards the merely intellectual part of it), consists in this accuracy. A well- educated gentleman may not know many languages, —may not be able to speak any but his own, —may have read very few books. But whatever language he knows, he knows precisely; whatever word he pronounces, he pronounces rightly; above all, he is learned in the PEERAGE of words; knows the words of true descent and ancient blood, at a glance, from words of modern canaille; remembers all their ancestry, their intermarriages, distant relationships, and the extent to which they were admitted, and offices they held, among the national noblesse of words at any time, and in any country. But an uneducated person may know, by memory, many languages, and talk them all, and yet truly know not a word of any, —not a word even of his own. An ordinarily clever and sensible seaman will be able to make his way ashore at most ports; yet he has only to speak a sentence of any language to be known for an illiterate person: so also the accent, or turn of expression of a single sentence, will at once mark a scholar. And this is so strongly felt, so conclusively admitted, by educated persons, that a false accent or a mistaken syllable is enough, in the parliament of any civilized nation, to assign to a man a certain degree of inferior standing for ever.

And this is right; but it is a pity that the accuracy insisted on is not greater, and required to a serious purpose. It is right that a false Latin quantity should excite a smile in the House of Commons; but it is wrong that a false English MEANING should NOT excite a frown there. Let the accent of words be watched; and closely: let their meaning be watched more closely still, and fewer will do the work. A few words well chosen, and distinguished, will do work that a thousand cannot, when every one is acting, equivocally, in the function of another. Yes; and words, if they are not watched, will do deadly work sometimes. There are masked words droning and skulking about us in Europe just now, —(there never were so many, owing to the spread of a shallow, blotching, blundering, infectious "information, " or rather deformation, everywhere, and to the teaching of catechisms and phrases at school instead of human meanings)—there are masked words abroad, I say, which nobody understands, but which everybody uses, and most people will also fight for, live for, or even die for, fancying they mean this or that, or the other, of things dear to them: for such words wear chameleon cloaks—"ground-lion" cloaks, of the colour of the ground of any man's fancy: on that ground they lie in wait, and rend them with a spring from it. There never were creatures of prey so mischievous, never diplomatists so cunning, never poisoners so deadly, as these masked words; they are the unjust stewards of all men's ideas: whatever fancy or favourite instinct a man most cherishes, he gives to his favourite masked word to take care of for him; the word at last comes to have an infinite power over him, —you cannot get at him but by its ministry.

And in languages so mongrel in breed as the English, there is a fatal power of equivocation put into men's hands, almost whether they will or no, in being able to use Greek or Latin words for an idea when they want it to be awful; and Saxon or otherwise common words when they want it to be vulgar. What a singular and salutary effect, for instance, would be produced on the minds of people who are in the habit of taking the Form of the "Word" they live by, for the Power of which that Word tells them, if we always either retained, or refused, the Greek form "biblos, " or "biblion, " as the right expression for "book"—instead of employing it only in the one instance in which we wish to give dignity to the idea, and translating it into English everywhere else. How wholesome it would be for many simple persons if, in such places (for instance) as Acts xix. 19, we retained the Greek expression, instead of translating it, and they had to read—"Many of them also which used curious arts, brought their bibles together, and burnt them before all men; and they counted the price of them, and found it fifty thousand pieces of silver"! Or if, on the other hand, we translated where we retain it, and always spoke of "The Holy Book, " instead of "Holy Bible, " it might come into more heads than it does at present, that the Word of God, by which the heavens were, of old, and by which they are now kept in store, {6} cannot be made a present of to anybody in morocco binding; nor sown on any wayside by help either of steam plough or steam press; but is nevertheless being offered to us daily, and by us with contumely refused; and sown in us daily, and by us, as instantly as may be, choked.

So, again, consider what effect has been produced on the English vulgar mind by the use of the sonorous Latin form "damno, " in translating the Greek [Greek text which cannot be reproduced], when people charitably wish to make it forcible; and the substitution of the temperate "condemn" for it, when they choose to keep it gentle; and what notable sermons have been preached by illiterate clergymen on—"He that believeth not shall be damned; " though they would shrink with horror from translating Heb. xi. 7, "The saving of his house, by which he damned the world, " or John viii. 10-11, "Woman, hath no man damned thee? She saith, No man, Lord. Jesus answered her, Neither do I damn thee: go and sin no more. " And divisions in the mind of Europe, which have cost seas of blood, and in the defence of which the noblest souls of men have been cast away in frantic desolation, countless as forest-leaves—though, in the heart of them, founded on deeper causes—have nevertheless been rendered practically possible, mainly, by the European adoption of the Greek word for a public meeting, "ecclesia, " to give peculiar respectability to such meetings, when held for religious purposes; and other collateral equivocations, such as the vulgar English one of using the word "Priest" as a contraction for "presbyter. "

Now, in order to deal with words rightly, this is the habit you must form. Nearly every word in your language has been first a word of some other language—of Saxon, German, French, Latin, or Greek; (not to speak of eastern and primitive dialects). And many words have been all these—that is to say, have been Greek first, Latin next, French or German next, and English last: undergoing a certain change of sense and use on the lips of each nation; but retaining a deep vital meaning, which all good scholars feel in employing them, even at this day. If you do not know the Greek alphabet, learn it; young or old—girl or boy—whoever you may be, if you think of reading seriously (which, of course, implies that you have some leisure at command), learn your Greek alphabet; then get good dictionaries of all these languages, and whenever you are in doubt about a word, hunt it down patiently. Read Max Muller's lectures thoroughly, to begin with; and, after that, never let a word escape you that looks suspicious. It is severe work; but you will find it, even at first, interesting, and at last endlessly amusing. And the general gain to your character, in power and precision, will be quite incalculable.

Mind, this does not imply knowing, or trying to know, Greek or Latin, or French. It takes a whole life to learn any language perfectly. But you can easily ascertain the meanings through which the English word has passed; and those which in a good writer's work it must still bear.

And now, merely for example's sake, I will, with your permission, read a few lines of a true book with you, carefully; and see what will come out of them. I will take a book perfectly known to you all. No English words are more familiar to us, yet few perhaps have been read with less sincerity. I will take these few following lines of Lycidas: -

"Last came, and last did go,
The pilot of the Galilean lake.
Two massy keys he bore of metals twain,
(The golden opes, the iron shuts amain,)
He shook his mitred locks, and stern bespake,
'How well could I have spared for thee, young swain,
Enow of such as for their bellies' sake
Creep, and intrude, and climb into the fold!
Of other care they little reckoning make,
Than how to scramble at the shearers' feast,
And shove away the worthy bidden guest;
Blind mouths! that scarce themselves know how to hold
A sheep-hook, or have learn'd aught else, the least
That to the faithful herdman's art belongs!
What recks it them? What need they? They are sped;
And when they list, their lean and flashy songs
Grate on their scrannel pipes of wretched straw;

The hungry sheep look up, and are not fed,
But, swoln with wind, and the rank mist they draw,
Rot inwardly, and foul contagion spread;
Besides what the grim wolf with privy paw
Daily devours apace, and nothing said.'"

Let us think over this passage, and examine its words.

First, is it not singular to find Milton assigning to St. Peter, not only his full episcopal function, but the very types of it which Protestants usually refuse most passionately? His "mitred" locks! Milton was no Bishop-lover; how comes St. Peter to be "mitred"? "Two massy keys he bore. " Is this, then, the power of the keys claimed by the Bishops of Rome? and is it acknowledged here by Milton only in a poetical licence, for the sake of its picturesqueness, that he may get the gleam of the golden keys to help his effect?

Do not think it. Great men do not play stage tricks with the doctrines of life and death: only little men do that. Milton means what he says; and means it with his might too—is going to put the whole strength of his spirit presently into the saying of it. For though not a lover of false bishops, he WAS a lover of true ones; and the Lake-pilot is here, in his thoughts, the type and head of true episcopal power. For Milton reads that text, "I will give unto thee the keys of the kingdom of heaven, " quite honestly. Puritan though he be, he would not blot it out of the book because there have been bad bishops; nay, in order to understand HIM, we must understand that verse first; it will not do to eye it askance, or whisper it under our breath, as if it were a weapon of an adverse sect. It is a solemn, universal assertion, deeply to be kept in mind by all sects. But perhaps we shall be better able to reason on it if we go on a little farther, and come back to it. For clearly this marked insistence on the power of the true episcopate is to make us feel more weightily what is to be charged against the false claimants of episcopate; or generally, against false claimants of power and rank in the body of the clergy; they who, "for their bellies' sake, creep, and intrude, and climb into the fold. "

Never think Milton uses those three words to fill up his verse, as a loose writer would. He needs all the three; —especially those three, and no more than those—"creep, " and "intrude, " and "climb; " no other words would or could serve the turn, and no more could be added. For they exhaustively comprehend the three classes, correspondent to the three characters, of men who dishonestly seek ecclesiastical power. First, those who "CREEP" into the fold; who do not care for office, nor name, but for secret influence, and do all things occultly and cunningly, consenting to any servility of office or conduct, so only that they may intimately discern, and unawares direct, the minds of men. Then those who "intrude" (thrust, that is) themselves into the fold, who by natural insolence of heart, and stout eloquence of tongue, and fearlessly perseverant self-assertion, obtain hearing and authority with the common crowd. Lastly, those who "climb, " who, by labour and learning, both stout and sound, but selfishly exerted in the cause of their own ambition, gain high dignities and authorities, and become "lords over the heritage, " though not "ensamples to the flock. "

Now go on: -

"Of other care they little reckoning make,
Than how to scramble at the shearers' feast.
BLIND MOUTHS—"

I pause again, for this is a strange expression; a broken metaphor, one might think, careless and unscholarly.

Not so: its very audacity and pithiness are intended to make us look close at the phrase and remember it. Those two monosyllables express the precisely accurate contraries of right character, in the two great offices of the Church—those of bishop and pastor.

A "Bishop" means "a person who sees. "

A "Pastor" means "a person who feeds. "

The most unbishoply character a man can have is therefore to be Blind.

The most unpastoral is, instead of feeding, to want to be fed, —to be a Mouth.

Take the two reverses together, and you have "blind mouths. " We may advisably follow out this idea a little. Nearly all the evils in the Church have arisen from bishops desiring POWER more than LIGHT. They want authority, not outlook. Whereas their real office is not to rule; though it may be vigorously to exhort and rebuke: it is the king's office to rule; the bishop's office is to OVERSEE the flock;

to number it, sheep by sheep; to be ready always to give full account of it. Now it is clear he cannot give account of the souls, if he has not so much as numbered the bodies, of his flock. The first thing, therefore, that a bishop has to do is at least to put himself in a position in which, at any moment, he can obtain the history, from childhood, of every living soul in his diocese, and of its present state. Down in that back street, Bill, and Nancy, knocking each other's teeth out! —Does the bishop know all about it? Has he his eye upon them? Has he HAD his eye upon them? Can he circumstantially explain to us how Bill got into the habit of beating Nancy about the head? If he cannot, he is no bishop, though he had a mitre as high as Salisbury steeple; he is no bishop, —he has sought to be at the helm instead of the masthead; he has no sight of things. "Nay, " you say, "it is not his duty to look after Bill in the back street. " What! the fat sheep that have full fleeces—you think it is only those he should look after while (go back to your Milton) "the hungry sheep look up, and are not fed, besides what the grim wolf, with privy paw" (bishops knowing nothing about it), "daily devours apace, and nothing said"?

"But that's not our idea of a bishop. " {7} Perhaps not; but it was St. Paul's; and it was Milton's. They may be right, or we may be; but we must not think we are reading either one or the other by putting our meaning into their words.

I go on.

"But swoln with wind, and the rank mist they draw. "

This is to meet the vulgar answer that "if the poor are not looked after in their bodies, they are in their souls; they have spiritual food."

And Milton says, "They have no such thing as spiritual food; they are only swollen with wind. " At first you may think that is a coarse type, and an obscure one. But again, it is a quite literally accurate one. Take up your Latin and Greek dictionaries, and find out the meaning of "Spirit. " It is only a contraction of the Latin word "breath, " and an indistinct translation of the Greek word for "wind. " The same word is used in writing, "The wind bloweth where it listeth; " and in writing, "So is every one that is born of the Spirit; " born of the BREATH, that is; for it means the breath of God, in soul and body. We have the true sense of it in our words "inspiration" and "expire. " Now, there are two kinds of breath with which the flock may be filled, —God's breath, and man's. The breath of God is health, and life, and peace to them, as the air of heaven is to the flocks on the hills; but man's breath—the word which HE calls spiritual, —is disease and contagion to them, as the fog of the fen. They rot inwardly with it; they are puffed up by it, as a dead body by the vapours of its own decomposition. This is literally true of all false religious teaching; the first and last, and fatalest sign of it, is that "puffing up. " Your converted children, who teach their parents; your converted convicts, who teach honest men; your converted dunces, who, having lived in cretinous stupefaction half their lives, suddenly awaking to the fact of there being a God, fancy themselves therefore His peculiar people and messengers; your sectarians of every species, small and great, Catholic or Protestant, of high church or low, in so far as they think themselves exclusively in the right and others wrong; and, pre-eminently, in every sect, those who hold that men can be saved by thinking rightly instead of doing rightly, by word instead of act, and wish instead of work; —these are the true fog children— clouds, these, without water; bodies, these, of putrescent vapour and skin, without blood or flesh: blown bag-pipes for the fiends to pipe with—corrupt, and corrupting, —" Swollen with wind, and the rank mist they draw. "

Lastly, let us return to the lines respecting the power of the keys, for now we can understand them. Note the difference between Milton and Dante in their interpretation of this power: for once, the latter is weaker in thought; he supposes BOTH the keys to be of the gate of heaven; one is of gold, the other of silver: they are given by St. Peter to the sentinel angel; and it is not easy to determine the meaning either of the substances of the three steps of the gate, or of the two keys. But Milton makes one, of gold, the key of heaven; the other, of iron, the key of the prison in which the wicked teachers are to be bound who "have taken away the key of knowledge, yet entered not in themselves. "

We have seen that the duties of bishop and pastor are to see, and feed; and of all who do so it is said, "He that watereth, shall be watered also himself. " But the reverse is truth also. He that watereth not, shall be WITHERED himself; and he that seeth not, shall himself be shut out of sight—shut into the perpetual prison- house. And that prison opens here, as well as hereafter: he who is to be bound in heaven must first be bound on earth. That command to the strong angels, of which the rock-apostle is the image, "Take him, and bind him hand and foot, and cast him out, " issues, in its measure, against the teacher, for every help withheld, and for every truth refused, and for every falsehood enforced; so that he is more strictly fettered the more he fetters, and farther outcast as he more and more misleads, till at last the bars of the iron cage close upon him, and as "the golden opes, the iron shuts amain. "

We have got something out of the lines, I think, and much more is yet to be found in them; but we have done enough by way of example of the kind of word-by-word examination of your author which is rightly called "reading; " watching every accent and expression, and putting ourselves always in the author's place, annihilating our own personality, and seeking to enter into his, so as to be able assuredly to say, "Thus Milton thought, " not "Thus I thought, in misreading Milton. " And by this process you will gradually come to attach less weight to your own "Thus I thought" at other times. You will begin to perceive that what YOU thought was a matter of no serious importance; —that your thoughts on any subject are not perhaps the clearest and wisest that could be arrived at thereupon: - in fact, that unless you are a very singular person, you cannot be said to have any "thoughts" at all; that you have no materials for them, in any serious matters; {8}—no right to "think, " but only to try to learn more of the facts. Nay, most probably all your life (unless, as I said, you are a singular person) you will have no legitimate right to an "opinion" on any business, except that instantly under your hand. What must of necessity be done, you can always find out, beyond question, how to do. Have you a house to keep in order, a commodity to sell, a field to plough, a ditch to cleanse? There need be no two opinions about these proceedings; it is at your peril if you have not much more than an "opinion" on the way to manage such matters. And also, outside of your own business, there are one or two subjects on which you are bound to have but one opinion. That roguery and lying are objectionable, and are instantly to be flogged out of the way whenever discovered; —that covetousness and love of quarrelling are dangerous dispositions even in children, and deadly dispositions in men and nations; —that, in the end, the God of heaven and earth loves active, modest, and kind people, and hates idle, proud, greedy, and cruel ones; —on these general facts you are bound to have but one, and that a very strong, opinion. For the rest, respecting religions, governments, sciences, arts, you will find that, on the whole, you can know NOTHING, —judge nothing; that the best you can do, even though you may be a well- educated person, is to be silent, and strive to be wiser every day, and to understand a little more of the thoughts of others, which so soon as you try to do honestly, you will discover that the thoughts even of the wisest are very little more than pertinent questions. To put the difficulty into a clear shape, and exhibit to you the grounds for INdecision, that is all they can generally do for you! — and well for them and for us, if indeed they are able "to mix the music with our thoughts and sadden us with heavenly doubts. " This writer, from whom I have been reading to you, is not among the first or wisest: he sees shrewdly as far as he sees, and therefore it is easy to find out its full meaning; but with the greater men, you cannot fathom their meaning; they do not even wholly measure it themselves, —it is so wide. Suppose I had asked you, for instance, to seek for Shakespeare's opinion, instead of Milton's on this matter of Church authority? —or for Dante's? Have any of you, at this instant, the least idea what either thought about it? Have you ever balanced the scene with the bishops in 'Richard III. ' against the character of Cranmer? the description of St. Francis and St. Dominic against that of him who made Virgil wonder to gaze upon him, —"disteso, tanto vilmente, nell' eterno esilio; " or of him whom Dante stood beside, "come 'l frate che confessa lo perfido assassin? " {9} Shakespeare and Alighieri knew men better than most of us, I presume! They were both in the midst of the main struggle between the temporal and spiritual powers. They had an opinion, we may guess. But where is it? Bring it into court! Put Shakespeare's or Dante's creed into articles, and send IT up for trial by the Ecclesiastical Courts!

You will not be able, I tell you again, for many and many a day, to come at the real purposes and teaching of these great men; but a very little honest study of them will enable you to perceive that what you took for your own "judgment" was mere chance prejudice, and drifted, helpless, entangled weed of castaway thought; nay, you will see that most men's minds are indeed little better than rough heath wilderness, neglected and stubborn, partly barren, partly overgrown with pestilent brakes, and venomous, wind-sown herbage of evil surmise; that the first thing you have to do for them, and yourself, is eagerly and scornfully to set fire to THIS; burn all the jungle into wholesome ash-heaps, and then plough and sow. All the true literary work before you, for life, must begin with obedience to that order, "Break up your fallow ground, and SOW NOT AMONG THORNS. "

II. {10} Having then faithfully listened to the great teachers, that you may enter into their Thoughts, you have yet this higher advance to make; —you have to enter into their Hearts. As you go to them first for clear sight, so you must stay with them, that you may share at last their just and mighty Passion. Passion, or "sensation. " I am not afraid of the word; still less of the thing. You have heard many outcries against sensation lately; but, I can tell you, it is not less sensation we want, but more. The ennobling difference between one man and another, —between one animal and another, —is precisely in this, that one feels more than another. If we were sponges, perhaps sensation might not be easily got for us; if we were earth-worms, liable at every instant to be cut in two by the spade, perhaps too much sensation might not be good for us. But being human creatures, IT IS good for us; nay, we are only human in so far as we are sensitive, and our honour is precisely in proportion to our passion.

You know I said of that great and pure society of the Dead, that it would allow "no vain or vulgar person to enter there. " What do you think I meant by a "vulgar" person? What do you yourselves mean by "vulgarity"? You will find it a fruitful subject of thought; but, briefly, the essence of all vulgarity lies in want of sensation. Simple and innocent vulgarity is merely an untrained and undeveloped bluntness of body and mind; but in true inbred vulgarity, there is a dreadful callousness, which, in extremity, becomes capable of every sort of bestial habit and crime, without fear, without pleasure, without horror, and without pity. It is in the blunt hand and the dead heart, in the diseased habit, in the hardened conscience, that men become vulgar; they are for ever vulgar, precisely in proportion as they are incapable of sympathy, —of quick understanding, —of all that, in deep insistence on the common, but most accurate term, may be called the "tact" or "touch-faculty, " of body and soul: that tact which the Mimosa has in trees, which the pure woman has above all creatures; —fineness and fulness of sensation, beyond reason; — the guide and sanctifier of reason itself. Reason can but determine what is true: - it is the God-given passion of humanity which alone can recognise what God has made good.

We come then to that great concourse of the Dead, not merely to know from them what is True, but chiefly to feel with them what is just. Now, to feel with them, we must be like them; and none of us can become that without pains. As the true knowledge is disciplined and tested knowledge, —not the first thought that comes, so the true passion is disciplined and tested passion, —not the first passion that comes. The first that come are the vain, the false, the treacherous; if you yield to them they will lead you wildly and far, in vain pursuit, in hollow enthusiasm, till you have no true purpose and no true passion left. Not that any feeling possible to humanity is in itself wrong, but only wrong when undisciplined. Its nobility is in its force and justice; it is wrong when it is weak, and felt for paltry cause. There is a mean wonder, as of a child who sees a juggler tossing golden balls; and this is base, if you will. But do you think that the wonder is ignoble, or the sensation less, with which every human soul is called to watch the golden balls of heaven tossed through the night by the Hand that made them? There is a mean curiosity, as of a child opening a forbidden door, or a servant prying into her master's business; —and a noble curiosity, questioning, in the front of danger, the source of the great river beyond the sand, —the place of the great continents beyond the sea; - -a nobler curiosity still, which questions of the source of the River of Life, and of the space of the Continent of Heaven, —things which "the angels desire to look into. " So the anxiety is ignoble, with which you linger over the course and catastrophe of an idle tale; but do you think the anxiety is less, or greater, with which you watch, or OUGHT to watch, the dealings of fate and destiny with the life of an agonized nation? Alas! it is the narrowness, selfishness, minuteness, of your sensation that you have to deplore in England at this day; —sensation which spends itself in bouquets and speeches: in revellings and junketings; in sham fights and gay puppet shows, while you can look on and see noble nations murdered, man by man, without an effort or a tear.

I said "minuteness" and "selfishness" of sensation, but it would have been enough to have said "injustice" or "unrighteousness" of sensation. For as in nothing is a gentleman better to be discerned from a vulgar person, so in nothing is a gentle nation (such nations have been) better to be discerned from a mob, than in this, —that their feelings are constant and just, results of due contemplation, and of equal thought. You can talk a mob into anything; its feelings may be—usually are—on the whole, generous and right; but it has no foundation for them, no hold of them; you may tease or tickle it into any, at your pleasure; it thinks by infection, for the most part, catching an opinion like a cold, and there is nothing so little that it will not roar itself wild about, when the fit is on; —nothing so great but it will forget in an hour, when the fit is past. But a gentleman's, or a gentle nation's, passions are just, measured, and continuous. A great nation, for instance, does not spend its entire national wits for a couple of months in weighing evidence of a single ruffian's having done a single murder; and for a couple of years see its own children murder each other by their thousands or tens of thousands a day, considering only what the effect is likely to be on the price of cotton, and caring no wise to determine which side of battle is in the wrong. Neither does a great nation send its poor little boys to jail for stealing six walnuts; and allow its bankrupts to steal their hundreds of thousands with a bow, and its bankers, rich with poor men's savings, to close their doors "under circumstances over which they have no control, " with a "by your leave; " and large landed estates to be bought by men who have made their money by going with armed steamers up and down the China Seas, selling opium at the cannon's mouth, and altering, for the benefit of the foreign nation, the common highwayman's demand of "your money OR your life, " into that of "your money AND your life. " Neither does a great nation allow the lives of its innocent poor to be parched out of them by fog fever, and rotted out of them by dunghill plague, for the sake of sixpence a life extra per week to its landlords; {11} and then debate, with drivelling tears, and diabolical sympathies, whether it ought not piously to save, and nursingly cherish, the lives of its murderers. Also, a great nation having made up its mind that hanging is quite the wholesomest process for its homicides in general, can yet with mercy distinguish between the degrees of guilt in homicides; and does not yelp like a pack of frost-pinched wolf-cubs on the blood-track of an unhappy crazed boy, or grey-haired clodpate Othello, "perplexed i' the extreme, " at the very moment that it is sending a Minister of the Crown to make polite speeches to a man who is bayoneting young girls in their fathers' sight, and killing noble youths in cool blood, faster than a country butcher kills lambs in spring. And, lastly, a great nation does not mock Heaven and its Powers, by pretending belief in a revelation which asserts the love of money to be the root of ALL evil, and declaring, at the same time, that it is actuated, and intends to be actuated, in all chief national deeds and measures, by no other love. {12}

My friends, I do not know why any of us should talk about reading. We want some sharper discipline than that of reading; but, at all events, be assured, we cannot read. No reading is possible for a people with its mind in this state. No sentence of any great writer is intelligible to them. It is simply and sternly impossible for the English public, at this moment, to understand any thoughtful writing, —so incapable of thought has it become in its insanity of avarice. Happily, our disease is, as yet, little worse than this incapacity of thought; it is not corruption of the inner nature; we ring true still, when anything strikes home to us; and though the idea that everything should "pay" has infected our every purpose so deeply, that even when we would play the good Samaritan, we never take out our two pence and give them to the host, without saying, "When I come again, thou shalt give me fourpence, " there is a capacity of noble passion left in our hearts' core. We show it in our work—in our war, —even in those unjust domestic affections which make us furious at a small private wrong, while we are polite to a boundless public one: we are still industrious to the last hour of the day, though we add the gambler's fury to the labourer's patience; we are still brave to the death, though incapable of discerning true cause for battle; and are still true in affection to our own flesh, to the death, as the sea-monsters are, and the rock- eagles. And there is hope for a nation while this can be still said of it. As long as it holds its life in its hand, ready to give it for its honour (though a foolish honour), for its love (though a selfish love), and for its business (though a base business), there is hope for it. But hope only; for this instinctive, reckless virtue cannot last. No nation can last, which has made a mob of itself, however generous at heart. It must discipline its passions, and direct them, or they will discipline it, one day, with scorpion whips. Above all, a nation cannot last as a money-making mob: it cannot with impunity, —it cannot with existence, —go on despising literature, despising science, despising art, despising nature, despising compassion, and concentrating its soul on Pence. Do you think these are harsh or wild words? Have patience with me but a little longer. I will prove their truth to you, clause by clause.

(I.) I say first we have despised literature. What do we, as a nation, care about books? How much do you think we spend altogether on our libraries, public or private, as compared with what we spend on our horses? If a man spends lavishly on his library, you call him mad—a bibliomaniac. But you never call any one a horsemaniac, though men ruin themselves every day by their horses, and you do not hear of people ruining themselves by their books. Or, to go lower still, how much do you think the contents of the book-shelves of the United Kingdom, public and private, would fetch, as compared with the contents of its wine-cellars? What position would its expenditure on literature take, as compared with its expenditure on luxurious eating? We talk of food for the mind, as of food for the body: now a good book contains such food inexhaustibly; it is a provision for life, and for the best part of us; yet how long most people would look at the best book before they would give the price of a large turbot for it? Though there have been men who have pinched their stomachs and bared their backs to buy a book, whose libraries were cheaper to them, I think, in the end, than most men's dinners are. We are few of us put to such trial, and more the pity; for, indeed, a precious thing is all the more precious to us if it has been won by work or economy; and if public libraries were half so costly as public dinners, or books cost the tenth part of what bracelets do, even foolish men and women might sometimes suspect there was good in reading, as well as in munching and sparkling: whereas the very cheapness of literature is making even wise people forget that if a book is worth reading, it is worth buying. No book is worth anything which is not worth MUCH; nor is it serviceable, until it has been read, and re-read, and loved, and loved again; and marked, so that you can refer to the passages you want in it, as a soldier can seize the weapon he needs in an armoury, or a housewife bring the spice she needs from her store. Bread of flour is good; but there is bread, sweet as honey, if we would eat it, in a good book; and the family must be poor indeed, which, once in their lives, cannot, for, such multipliable barley-loaves, pay their baker's bill. We call ourselves a rich nation, and we are filthy and foolish enough to thumb each other's books out of circulating libraries!

(II.) I say we have despised science. "What! " you exclaim, "are we not foremost in all discovery, {13} and is not the whole world giddy by reason, or unreason, of our inventions? " Yes; but do you suppose that is national work? That work is all done IN SPITE OF the nation; by private people's zeal and money. We are glad enough, indeed, to make our profit of science; we snap up anything in the way of a scientific bone that has meat on it, eagerly enough; but if the scientific man comes for a bone or a crust to US, that is another story. What have we publicly done for science? We are obliged to know what o'clock it is, for the safety of our ships, and therefore we pay for an observatory; and we allow ourselves, in the person of our Parliament, to be annually tormented into doing something, in a slovenly way, for the British Museum; sullenly apprehending that to be a place for keeping stuffed birds in, to amuse our children. If anybody will pay for their own telescope, and resolve another nebula, we cackle over the discernment as if it were our own; if one in ten thousand of our hunting squires suddenly perceives that the earth was indeed made to be something else than a portion for foxes, and burrows in it himself, and tells us where the gold is, and where the coals, we understand that there is some use in that; and very properly knight him: but is the accident of his having found out how to employ himself usefully any credit to US? (The negation of such discovery among his brother squires may perhaps be some discredit to us, if we would consider of it.) But if you doubt these generalities, here is one fact for us all to meditate upon, illustrative of our love of science. Two years ago there was a collection of the fossils of Solenhofen to be sold in Bavaria; the best in existence, containing many specimens unique for perfectness, and one unique as an example of a species (a whole kingdom of unknown living creatures being announced by that fossil). This collection, of which the mere market worth, among private buyers, would probably have been some thousand or twelve hundred pounds, was offered to the English nation for seven hundred: but we would not give seven hundred, and the whole series would have been in the Munich Museum at this moment, if Professor Owen {14} had not, with loss of his own time, and patient tormenting of the British public in person of its representatives, got leave to give four hundred pounds at once, and himself become answerable for the other three! which the said public will doubtless pay him eventually, but sulkily, and caring nothing about the matter all the while; only always ready to cackle if any credit comes of it. Consider, I beg of you, arithmetically, what this fact means. Your annual expenditure for public purposes, (a third of it for military apparatus,) is at least 50 millions. Now 700L. is to 50,000,000L. roughly, as seven pence to two thousand pounds. Suppose, then, a gentleman of unknown income, but whose wealth was to be conjectured from the fact that he spent two thousand a year on his park-walls and footmen only, professes himself fond of science; and that one of his servants comes eagerly to tell him that an unique collection of fossils, giving clue to a new era of creation, is to be had for the sum of seven pence sterling; and that the gentleman who is fond of science, and spends two thousand a year on his park, answers, after keeping his servant waiting several months, "Well! I'll give you fourpence for them, if you will be answerable for the extra threepence yourself, till next year! "

(III.) I say you have despised Art! "What! " you again answer, "have we not Art exhibitions, miles long? and do we not pay thousands of pounds for single pictures? and have we not Art schools and institutions, —more than ever nation had before? " Yes, truly, but all that is for the sake of the shop. You would fain sell canvas as well as coals, and crockery as well as iron; you would take every other nation's bread out of its mouth if you could; {15} not being able to do that, your ideal of life is to stand in the thoroughfares of the world, like Ludgate apprentices, screaming to every passer-by, "What d'ye lack? " You know nothing of your own faculties or circumstances; you fancy that, among your damp, flat, fat fields of clay, you can have as quick art-fancy as the Frenchman among his bronzed vines, or the Italian under his volcanic cliffs; — that Art may be learned, as book-keeping is, and when learned, will give you more books to keep. You care for pictures, absolutely, no more than you do for the bills pasted on your dead walls. There is always room on the walls for the bills to be read, —never for the pictures to be seen. You do not know what pictures you have (by repute) in the country, nor whether they are false or true, nor whether they are taken care of or not; in foreign countries, you calmly see the noblest existing pictures in the world rotting in abandoned wreck—(in Venice you saw the Austrian guns deliberately pointed at the palaces containing them), and if you heard that all the fine pictures in Europe were made into sand-bags to-morrow on the Austrian forts, it would not trouble you so much as the chance of a brace or two of game less in your own bags, in a day's shooting. That is your national love of Art.

(IV.) You have despised Nature; that is to say, all the deep and sacred sensations of natural scenery. The French revolutionists made stables of the cathedrals of France; you have made race-courses of the cathedrals of the earth. Your ONE conception of pleasure is to drive in railroad carriages round their aisles, and eat off their altars. {16} You have put a railroad-bridge over the falls of Schaffhausen. You have tunnelled the cliffs of Lucerne by Tell's chapel; you have destroyed the Clarens shore of the Lake of Geneva; there is not a quiet valley in England that you have not filled with bellowing fire; there is no particle left of English land which you have not trampled coal ashes into {17}—nor any foreign city in which the spread of your presence is not marked among its fair old streets and happy gardens by a consuming white leprosy of new hotels and perfumers' shops: the Alps themselves, which your own poets used to love so reverently, you look upon as soaped poles in a bear- garden, which you set yourselves to climb and slide down again, with "shrieks of delight. " When you are past shrieking, having no human articulate voice to say you are glad with, you fill the quietude of their valleys with gunpowder blasts, and rush home, red with cutaneous eruption of conceit, and voluble with convulsive hiccough of self-satisfaction. I think nearly the two sorrowfullest spectacles I have ever seen in humanity, taking the deep inner significance of them, are the English mobs in the valley of Chamouni, amusing themselves with firing rusty howitzers; and the Swiss vintagers of Zurich expressing their Christian thanks for the gift of the vine, by assembling in knots in the "towers of the vineyards, " and slowly loading and firing horse-pistols from morning till evening. It is pitiful, to have dim conceptions of duty; more pitiful, it seems to me, to have conceptions like these, of mirth.

Lastly. You despise compassion. There is no need of words of mine for proof of this. I will merely print one of the newspaper paragraphs which I am in the habit of cutting out and throwing into my store-drawer; here is one from a 'Daily Telegraph' of an early date this year (1867); (date which, though by me carelessly left unmarked, is easily discoverable; for on the back of the slip there is the announcement that "yesterday the seventh of the special services of this year was performed by the Bishop of Ripon in St. Paul's";) it relates only one of such facts as happen now daily; this by chance having taken a form in which it came before the coroner. I will print the paragraph in red. Be sure, the facts themselves are written in that colour, in a book which we shall all OF us, literate or illiterate, have to read our page of, some day.

An inquiry was held on Friday by Mr. Richards, deputy coroner, at the White Horse Tavern, Christ Church, Spitalfields, respecting the death of Michael Collins, aged 58 years. Mary Collins, a miserable-looking woman, said that she lived with the deceased and his son in a room at 2, Cobb's Court, Christ Church. Deceased was a "translator" of boots. Witness went out and bought old boots; deceased and his son made them into good ones, and then witness sold them for what she could get at the shops, which was very little indeed. Deceased and his son used to work night and day to try and get a little bread and tea, and pay for the room (2S. a week), so as to keep the home together. On Friday-night-week deceased got up from his bench and began to shiver. He threw down the boots, saying, "Somebody else must finish them when I am gone, for I can do no more. " There was no fire, and he said, "I would be better if I was warm. " Witness therefore took two pairs of translated boots {18} to sell at the shop, but she could only get 14D. for the two pairs, for the people at the shop said, "We must have our profit. " Witness got 14lb. of coal, and a little tea and bread. Her son sat up the whole night to make the "translations, " to get money, but deceased died on Saturday morning. The family never had enough to eat. —Coroner: "It seems to me deplorable that you did not go into the workhouse. " Witness: "We wanted the comforts of our little home. " A juror asked what the comforts were, for he only saw a little straw in the corner of the room, the windows of which were broken. The witness began to cry, and said that they had a quilt and other little things. The deceased said he never would go into the workhouse. In summer, when the season was good, they sometimes made as much as 10S. profit in the week. They then always saved towards the next week, which was generally a bad one. In winter they made not half so much. For three years they had been getting from bad to worse. — Cornelius Collins said that he had assisted his father since 1847. They used to work so far into the night that both nearly lost their eyesight. Witness now had a film over his eyes. Five years ago deceased applied to the parish for aid. The relieving officer gave him a 4lb. loaf, and told him if he came again he should "get the stones. " {19} That disgusted deceased, and he would have nothing to do with them since. They got worse and worse until last Friday week, when they had not even a half-penny to buy a candle. Deceased then lay down on the straw, and said he could not live till morning. —A juror: "You are dying of starvation yourself, and you ought to go into the house until the summer. "— Witness: "If we went in we should die. When we come out in the summer we should be like people dropped from the sky. No one would know us, and we would not have even a room. I could work now if I had food, for my sight would get better. " Dr. G. P. Walker said deceased died from syncope, from exhaustion from want of food. The deceased had had no bedclothes. For four months he had had nothing but bread to eat. There was not a particle of fat in the body. There was no disease, but, if there had been medical attendance, he might have survived the syncope or fainting. The Coroner having remarked upon the painful nature of the case, the jury returned the following verdict: "That deceased died from exhaustion from want of food and the common necessaries of life; also through want of medical aid. "

"Why would witness not go into the workhouse? " you ask. Well, the poor seem to have a prejudice against the workhouse which the rich have not; for of course everyone who takes a pension from Government goes into the workhouse on a grand scale: {20} only the workhouses for the rich do not involve the idea of work, and should be called play-houses. But the poor like to die independently, it appears; perhaps if we made the play-houses for them pretty and pleasant enough, or gave them their pensions at home, and allowed them a little introductory peculation with the public money, their minds might be reconciled to the conditions. Meantime, here are the facts: we make our relief either so insulting to them, or so painful, that they rather die than take it at our hands; or, for third alternative, we leave them so untaught and foolish that they starve like brute creatures, wild and dumb, not knowing what to do, or what to ask. I say, you despise compassion; if you did not, such a newspaper paragraph would be as impossible in a Christian country as a deliberate assassination permitted in its public streets. {21} "Christian, " did I say? Alas! if we were but wholesomely UN-Christian, it would be impossible: it is our imaginary Christianity that helps us to commit these crimes, for we revel and luxuriate in our faith, for the lewd sensation of it; dressing IT up, like everything else, in fiction. The dramatic Christianity of the organ and aisle, of dawn-service and twilight-revival—the Christianity, which we do not fear to mix the mockery of, pictorially, with our play about the devil, in our Satanellas, —Roberts, —Fausts; chanting hymns through traceried windows for background effect, and artistically modulating the "Dio" through variation on variation of mimicked prayer: (while we distribute tracts, next day, for the benefit of uncultivated swearers, upon what we suppose to be the signification of the Third Commandment; -) this gas-lighted, and gas- inspired Christianity, we are triumphant in, and draw back the hem of our robes from the touch of the heretics who dispute it. But to do a piece of common Christian righteousness in a plain English word or deed; to make Christian law any rule of life, and found one National act or hope thereon, —we know too well what our faith comes to for that! You might sooner get lightning out of incense smoke than true action or passion out of your modern English religion. You had better get rid of the smoke, and the organ pipes, both: leave them, and the Gothic windows, and the painted glass, to the property man; give up your carburetted hydrogen ghost in one healthy expiration, and look after Lazarus at the doorstep. For there is a true Church wherever one hand meets another helpfully, and that is the only holy or Mother Church which ever was, or ever shall be.

All these pleasures then, and all these virtues, I repeat, you nationally despise. You have, indeed, men among you who do not; by whose work, by whose strength, by whose life, by whose death, you live, and never thank them. Your wealth, your amusement, your pride, would all be alike impossible, but for those whom you scorn or forget. The policeman, who is walking up and down the black lane all night to watch the guilt you have created there; and may have his brains beaten out, and be maimed for life, at any moment, and never be thanked; the sailor wrestling with the sea's rage; the quiet student poring over his book or his vial; the common worker, without praise, and nearly without bread, fulfilling his task as your horses drag your carts, hopeless, and spurned of all: these are the men by whom England lives; but they are not the nation; they are only the body and nervous force of it, acting still from old habit in a convulsive perseverance, while the mind is gone. Our National wish and purpose are only to be amused; our National religion is the performance of church ceremonies, and preaching of soporific truth (or untruths) to keep the mob quietly at work, while we amuse ourselves; and the necessity for this amusement is fastening on us, as a feverous disease of parched throat and wandering eyes—senseless, dissolute, merciless. How literally that word DIS-Ease, the Negation and impossibility of Ease, expresses the entire moral state of our English Industry and its Amusements!

When men are rightly occupied, their amusement grows out of their work, as the colour-petals out of a fruitful flower; —when they are faithfully helpful and compassionate, all their emotions become steady, deep, perpetual, and vivifying to the soul as the natural pulse to the body. But now, having no true business, we pour our whole masculine energy into the false business of money-making; and having no true emotion, we must have false emotions dressed up for us to play with, not innocently, as children with dolls, but guiltily and darkly, as the idolatrous Jews with their pictures on cavern walls, which men had to dig to detect. The justice we do not execute, we mimic in the novel and on the stage; for the beauty we destroy in nature, we substitute the metamorphosis of the pantomime, and (the human nature of us imperatively requiring awe and sorrow of SOME kind) for the noble grief we should have borne with our fellows, and the pure tears we should have wept with them, we gloat over the pathos of the police court, and gather the night-dew of the grave.

It is difficult to estimate the true significance of these things; the facts are frightful enough; —the measure of national fault involved in them is perhaps not as great as it would at first seem. We permit, or cause, thousands of deaths daily, but we mean no harm; we set fire to houses, and ravage peasants' fields, yet we should be sorry to find we had injured anybody. We are still kind at heart; still capable of virtue, but only as children are. Chalmers, at the end of his long life, having had much power with the public, being plagued in some serious matter by a reference to "public opinion, " uttered the impatient exclamation, "The public is just a great baby! " And the reason that I have allowed all these graver subjects of thought to mix themselves up with an inquiry into methods of reading, is that, the more I see of our national faults or miseries, the more they resolve themselves into conditions of childish illiterateness and want of education in the most ordinary habits of thought. It is, I repeat, not vice, not selfishness, not dulness of brain, which we have to lament; but an unreachable schoolboy's recklessness, only differing from the true schoolboy's in its incapacity of being helped, because it acknowledges no master.

There is a curious type of us given in one of the lovely, neglected works of the last of our great painters. It is a drawing of Kirkby Lonsdale churchyard, and of its brook, and valley, and hills, and folded morning sky beyond. And unmindful alike of these, and of the dead who have left these for other valleys and for other skies, a group of schoolboys have piled their little books upon a grave, to strike them off with stones. So, also, we play with the words of the dead that would teach us, and strike them far from us with our bitter, reckless will; little thinking that those leaves which the wind scatters had been piled, not only upon a gravestone, but upon the seal of an enchanted vault—nay, the gate of a great city of sleeping kings, who would awake for us and walk with us, if we knew but how to call them by their names. How often, even if we lift the marble entrance gate, do we but wander among those old kings in their repose, and finger the robes they lie in, and stir the crowns on their foreheads; and still they are silent to us, and seem but a dusty imagery; because we know not the incantation of the heart that would wake them; —which, if they once heard, they would start up to meet us in their power of long ago, narrowly to look upon us, and consider us; and, as the fallen kings of Hades meet the newly fallen, saying, "Art thou also become weak as we—art thou also become one of us? " so would these kings, with their undimmed, unshaken diadems, meet us, saying, "Art thou also become pure and mighty of heart as we—art thou also become one of us? "

Mighty of heart, mighty of mind—"magnanimous"—to be this, is indeed to be great in life; to become this increasingly, is, indeed, to "advance in life, "—in life itself—not in the trappings of it. My friends, do you remember that old Scythian custom, when the head of a house died? How he was dressed in his finest dress, and set in his chariot, and carried about to his friends' houses; and each of them placed him at his table's head, and all feasted in his presence? Suppose it were offered to you in plain words, as it IS offered to you in dire facts, that you should gain this Scythian honour, gradually, while you yet thought yourself alive. Suppose the offer were this: You shall die slowly; your blood shall daily grow cold, your flesh petrify, your heart beat at last only as a rusted group of iron valves. Your life shall fade from you, and sink through the earth into the ice of Caina; but, day by day, your body shall be dressed more gaily, and set in higher chariots, and have more orders on its breast—crowns on its head, if you will. Men shall bow before it, stare and shout round it, crowd after it up and down the streets; build palaces for it, feast with it at their tables' heads all the night long; your soul shall stay enough within it to know what they do, and feel the weight of the golden dress on its shoulders, and the furrow of the crown-edge on the skull; —no more. Would you take the offer, verbally made by the death-angel? Would the meanest among us take it, think you? Yet practically and verily we grasp at it, every one of us, in a measure; many of us grasp at it in its fulness of horror. Every man accepts it, who desires to advance in life without knowing what life is; who means only that he is to get more horses, and more footmen, and more fortune, and more public honour, and—NOT more personal soul. He only is advancing in life, whose heart is getting softer, whose blood warmer, whose brain quicker, whose spirit is entering into Living {22} peace. And the men who have this life in them are the true lords or kings of the earth—they, and they only. All other kingships, so far as they are true, are only the practical issue and expression of theirs; if less than this, they are either dramatic royalties, —costly shows, set off, indeed, with real jewels, instead of tinsel—but still only the toys of nations; or else they are no royalties at all, but tyrannies, or the mere active and practical issue of national folly; for which reason I have said of them elsewhere, "Visible governments are the toys of some nations, the diseases of others, the harness of some, the burdens of more. "

But I have no words for the wonder with which I hear Kinghood still spoken of, even among thoughtful men, as if governed nations were a personal property, and might be bought and sold, or otherwise acquired, as sheep, of whose flesh their king was to feed, and whose fleece he was to gather; as if Achilles' indignant epithet of base kings, "people-eating, " were the constant and proper title of all monarchs; and the enlargement of a king's dominion meant the same thing as the increase of a private man's estate! Kings who think so, however powerful, can no more be the true kings of the nation than gadflies are the kings of a horse; they suck it, and may drive it wild, but do not guide it. They, and their courts, and their armies are, if one could see clearly, only a large species of marsh mosquito, with bayonet proboscis and melodious, band-mastered trumpeting, in the summer air; the twilight being, perhaps, sometimes fairer, but hardly more wholesome, for its glittering mists of midge companies. The true kings, meanwhile, rule quietly, if at all, and hate ruling; too many of them make "il gran rifiuto; " and if they do not, the mob, as soon as they are likely to become useful to it, is pretty sure to make ITS "gran rifiuto" of THEM.

Yet the visible king may also be a true one, some day, if ever day comes when he will estimate his dominion by the FORCE of it, —not the geographical boundaries. It matters very little whether Trent cuts you a cantel out here, or Rhine rounds you a castle less there. But it does matter to you, king of men, whether you can verily say to this man, "Go, " and he goeth; and to another, "Come, " and he cometh. Whether you can turn your people, as you can Trent—and where it is that you bid them come, and where go. It matters to you, king of men, whether your people hate you, and die by you, or love you, and live by you. You may measure your dominion by multitudes, better than by miles; and count degrees of love- latitude, not from, but to, a wonderfully warm and infinite equator.

Measure! —nay, you cannot measure. Who shall measure the difference between the power of those who "do and teach, " and who are greatest in the kingdoms of earth, as of heaven—and the power of those who undo, and consume—whose power, at the fullest, is only the power of the moth and the rust? Strange! to think how the Moth-kings lay up treasures for the moth; and the Rust-kings, who are to their peoples' strength as rust to armour, lay up treasures for the rust; and the Robber-kings, treasures for the robber; but how few kings have ever laid up treasures that needed no guarding—treasures of which, the more thieves there were, the better! Broidered robe, only to be rent; helm and sword, only to be dimmed; jewel and gold, only to be scattered; —there have been three kinds of kings who have gathered these. Suppose there ever should arise a Fourth order of kings, who had read, in some obscure writing of long ago, that there was a Fourth kind of treasure, which the jewel and gold could not equal, neither should it be valued with pure gold. A web made fair in the weaving, by Athena's shuttle; an armour, forged in divine fire by Vulcanian force; a gold to be mined in the very sun's red heart, where he sets over the Delphian cliffs; —deep-pictured tissue; —impenetrable armour; —potable gold! —the three great Angels of Conduct, Toil, and Thought, still calling to us, and waiting at the posts of our doors, to lead us, with their winged power, and guide us, with their unerring eyes, by the path which no fowl knoweth, and which the vulture's eye has not seen! Suppose kings should ever arise, who heard and believed this word, and at last gathered and brought forth treasures of—Wisdom—for their people?

Think what an amazing business THAT would be! How inconceivable, in the state of our present national wisdom! That we should bring up our peasants to a book exercise instead of a bayonet exercise! — organise, drill, maintain with pay, and good generalship, armies of thinkers, instead of armies of stabbers! —find national amusement in reading-rooms as well as rifle-grounds; give prizes for a fair shot at a fact, as well as for a leaden splash on a target. What an absurd idea it seems, put fairly in words, that the wealth of the capitalists of civilised nations should ever come to support literature instead of war!

Have yet patience with me, while I read you a single sentence out of the only book, properly to be called a book, that I have yet written myself, the one that will stand (if anything stand), surest and longest of all work of mine.

"It is one very awful form of the operation of wealth in Europe that it is entirely capitalists' wealth which supports unjust wars. Just wars do not need so much money to support them; for most of the men who wage such, wage them gratis; but for an unjust war, men's bodies and souls have both to be bought; and the best tools of war for them besides, which make such war costly to the maximum; not to speak of the cost of base fear, and angry suspicion, between nations which have not grace nor honesty enough in all their multitudes to buy an hour's peace of mind with; as, at present, France and England, purchasing of each other ten millions sterling worth of consternation, annually (a remarkably light crop, half thorns and half aspen leaves, sown, reaped, and granaried by the 'science' of the modern political economist, teaching covetousness instead of truth). And, all unjust war being supportable, if not by pillage of the enemy, only by loans from capitalists, these loans are repaid by subsequent taxation of the people, who appear to have no will in the matter, the capitalists' will being the primary root of the war; but its real root is the covetousness of the whole nation, rendering it incapable of faith, frankness, or justice, and bringing about, therefore, in due time, his own separate loss and punishment to each person. "

France and England literally, observe, buy PANIC of each other; they pay, each of them, for ten thousand-thousand-pounds'-worth of terror, a year. Now suppose, instead of buying these ten millions' worth of panic annually, they made up their minds to be at peace with each other, and buy ten millions' worth of knowledge annually; and that each nation spent its ten thousand thousand pounds a year in founding royal libraries, royal art galleries, royal museums, royal gardens, and places of rest. Might it not be better somewhat for both French and English?

It will be long, yet, before that comes to pass. Nevertheless, I hope it will not be long before royal or national libraries will be founded in every considerable city, with a royal series of books in them; the same series in every one of them, chosen books, the best in every kind, prepared for that national series in the most perfect way possible; their text printed all on leaves of equal size, broad of margin, and divided into pleasant volumes, light in the hand, beautiful, and strong, and thorough as examples of binders' work; and that these great libraries will be accessible to all clean and orderly persons at all times of the day and evening; strict law being enforced for this cleanliness and quietness.

I could shape for you other plans, for art-galleries, and for natural history galleries, and for many precious—many, it seems to me, needful—things; but this book plan is the easiest and needfullest, and would prove a considerable tonic to what we call our British constitution, which has fallen dropsical of late, and has an evil thirst, and evil hunger, and wants healthier feeding. You have got its corn laws repealed for it; try if you cannot get corn laws established for it, dealing in a better bread; —bread made of that old enchanted Arabian grain, the Sesame, which opens doors; - -doors not of robbers', but of Kings' Treasuries.

LECTURE II. —LILIES OF QUEENS' GARDENS

"Be thou glad, oh thirsting Desert; let the desert be made cheerful, and bloom as the lily; and the barren places of Jordan shall run wild with wood. "—ISAIAH XXXV. I. (Septuagint.)

It will, perhaps, be well, as this Lecture is the sequel of one previously given, that I should shortly state to you my general intention in both. The questions specially proposed to you in the first, namely, How and What to Read, rose out of a far deeper one, which it was my endeavour to make you propose earnestly to yourselves, namely, WHY to Read. I want you to feel, with me, that whatever advantages we possess in the present day in the diffusion of education and of literature, can only be rightly used by any of us when we have apprehended clearly what education is to lead to, and literature to teach. I wish you to see that both well-directed moral training and well-chosen reading lead to the possession of a power over the ill-guided and illiterate, which is, according to the measure of it, in the truest sense, KINGLY; conferring indeed the purest kingship that can exist among men: too many other kingships (however distinguished by visible insignia or material power) being either spectral, or tyrannous; —spectral—that is to say, aspects and shadows only of royalty, hollow as death, and which only the "likeness of a kingly crown have on: " or else—tyrannous—that is to say, substituting their own will for the law of justice and love by which all true kings rule.

There is, then, I repeat—and as I want to leave this idea with you, I begin with it, and shall end with it—only one pure kind of kingship; an inevitable and eternal kind, crowned or not; the kingship, namely, which consists in a stronger moral state, and a truer thoughtful state, than that of others; enabling you, therefore, to guide, or to raise them. Observe that word "State; " we have got into a loose way of using it. It means literally the standing and stability of a thing; and you have the full force of it in the derived word "statue"—"the immovable thing. " A king's majesty or "state, " then, and the right of his kingdom to be called a state, depends on the movelessness of both: - without tremor, without quiver of balance; established and enthroned upon a foundation of eternal law which nothing can alter, nor overthrow.

Believing that all literature and all education are only useful so far as they tend to confirm this calm, beneficent, and THEREFORE kingly, power—first, over ourselves, and, through ourselves, over all around us, —I am now going to ask you to consider with me farther, what special portion or kind of this royal authority, arising out of noble education, may rightly be possessed by women; and how far they also are called to a true queenly power, —not in their households merely, but over all within their sphere. And in what sense, if they rightly understood and exercised this royal or gracious influence, the order and beauty induced by such benignant power would justify us in speaking of the territories over which each of them reigned, as "Queens' Gardens. "

And here, in the very outset, we are met by a far deeper question, which—strange though this may seem—remains among many of us yet quite undecided in spite of its infinite importance.

We cannot determine what the queenly power of women should be, until we are agreed what their ordinary power should be. We cannot consider how education may fit them for any widely extending duty, until we are agreed what is their true constant duty. And there never was a time when wilder words were spoken, or more vain imagination permitted, respecting this question—quite vital to all social happiness. The relations of the womanly to the manly nature, their different capacities of intellect or of virtue, seem never to have been yet estimated with entire consent. We hear of the "mission" and of the "rights" of Woman, as if these could ever be separate from the mission and the rights of Man—as if she and her lord were creatures of independent kind, and of irreconcilable claim. This, at least, is wrong. And not less wrong—perhaps even more foolishly wrong (for I will anticipate thus far what I hope to prove)—is the idea that woman is only the shadow and attendant image of her lord, owing him a thoughtless and servile obedience, and supported altogether in her weakness by the pre-eminence of his fortitude.

This, I say, is the most foolish of all errors respecting her who was made to be the helpmate of man. As if he could be helped effectively by a shadow, or worthily by a slave!

Let us try, then, whether we cannot get at some clear and harmonious idea (it must be harmonious if it is true) of what womanly mind and virtue are in power and office, with respect to man's; and how their relations, rightly accepted, aid and increase the vigour and honour and authority of both.

And now I must repeat one thing I said in the last lecture: namely, that the first use of education was to enable us to consult with the wisest and the greatest men on all points of earnest difficulty. That to use books rightly, was to go to them for help: to appeal to them, when our own knowledge and power of thought failed: to be led by them into wider sight, —purer conception, —than our own, and receive from them the united sentence of the judges and councils of all time, against our solitary and unstable opinion.

Let us do this now. Let us see whether the greatest, the wisest, the purest-hearted of all ages are agreed in any wise on this point: let us hear the testimony they have left respecting what they held to be the true dignity of woman, and her mode of help to man.

And first let us take Shakespeare.

Note broadly in the outset, Shakespeare has no heroes; —he has only heroines. There is not one entirely heroic figure in all his plays, except the slight sketch of Henry the Fifth, exaggerated for the purposes of the stage; and the still slighter Valentine in The Two Gentlemen of Verona. In his laboured and perfect plays you have no hero. Othello would have been one, if his simplicity had not been so great as to leave him the prey of every base practice round him; but he is the only example even approximating to the heroic type. Coriolanus—Caesar—Antony stand in flawed strength, and fall by their vanities; —Hamlet is indolent, and drowsily speculative; Romeo an impatient boy; the Merchant of Venice languidly submissive to adverse fortune; Kent, in King Lear, is entirely noble at heart, but too rough and unpolished to be of true use at the critical time, and he sinks into the office of a servant only. Orlando, no less noble, is yet the despairing toy of chance, followed, comforted, saved by Rosalind. Whereas there is hardly a play that has not a perfect woman in it, steadfast in grave hope, and errorless purpose: Cordelia, Desdemona, Isabella, Hermione, Imogen, Queen Catherine, Perdita, Sylvia, Viola, Rosalind, Helena, and last, and perhaps loveliest, Virgilia, are all faultless; conceived in the highest heroic type of humanity.

Then observe, secondly,

The catastrophe of every play is caused always by the folly or fault of a man; the redemption, if there be any, is by the wisdom and virtue of a woman, and, failing that, there is none. The catastrophe of King Lear is owing to his own want of judgment, his impatient vanity, his misunderstanding of his children; the virtue of his one true daughter would have saved him from all the injuries of the others, unless he had cast her away from him; as it is, she all but saves him.

Of Othello I need not trace the tale; —nor the one weakness of his so mighty love; nor the inferiority of his perceptive intellect to that even of the second woman character in the play, the Emilia who dies in wild testimony against his error: -

"Oh, murderous coxcomb! what should such a fool Do with so good a wife? "

In Romeo and Juliet, the wise and brave stratagem of the wife is brought to ruinous issue by the reckless impatience of her husband. In Winter's Tale, and in Cymbeline, the happiness and existence of two princely households, lost through long years, and imperilled to the death by the folly and obstinacy of the husbands, are redeemed at last by the queenly patience and wisdom of the wives. In Measure for Measure, the foul injustice of the judge, and the foul cowardice of the brother, are opposed to the victorious truth and adamantine purity of a woman. In Coriolanus, the mother's counsel, acted upon in time, would have saved her son from all evil; his momentary forgetfulness of it is his ruin; her prayer, at last granted, saves him— not, indeed, from death, but from the curse of living as the destroyer of his country.

And what shall I say of Julia, constant against the fickleness of a lover who is a mere wicked child? —of Helena, against the petulance and insult of a careless youth? —of the patience of Hero, the passion of Beatrice, and the calmly devoted wisdom of the "unlessoned girl, " who appears among the helplessness, the blindness, and the vindictive passions of men, as a gentle angel, bringing courage and safety by her presence, and defeating the worst malignities of crime by what women are fancied most to fail in, — precision and accuracy of thought.

Observe, further, among all the principal figures in Shakespeare's plays, there is only one weak woman—Ophelia; and it is because she fails Hamlet at the critical moment, and is not, and cannot in her nature be, a guide to him when he needs her most, that all the bitter catastrophe follows. Finally, though there are three wicked women among the principal figures—Lady Macbeth, Regan, and Goneril- -they are felt at once to be frightful exceptions to the ordinary laws of life; fatal in their influence also, in proportion to the power for good which they have abandoned.

Such, in broad light, is Shakespeare's testimony to the position and character of women in human life. He represents them as infallibly faithful and wise counsellors, —incorruptibly just and pure examples—strong always to sanctify, even when they cannot save.

Not as in any wise comparable in knowledge of the nature of man, — still less in his understanding of the causes and courses of fate, — but only as the writer who has given us the broadest view of the conditions and modes of ordinary thought in modern society, I ask you next to receive the witness of Walter Scott.

I put aside his merely romantic prose writings as of no value, and though the early romantic poetry is very beautiful, its testimony is of no weight, other than that of a boy's ideal. But his true works, studied from Scottish life, bear a true witness; and in the whole range of these, there are but three men who reach the heroic type {23}—Dandie Dinmont, Rob Roy, and Claverhouse; of these, one is a border farmer; another a freebooter; the third a soldier in a bad cause. And these touch the ideal of heroism only in their courage and faith, together with a strong, but uncultivated, or mistakenly applied, intellectual power; while his younger men are the gentlemanly play-things of fantastic fortune, and only by aid (or accident) of that fortune, survive, not vanquish, the trials they involuntarily sustain. Of any disciplined, or consistent character, earnest in a purpose wisely conceived, or dealing with forms of hostile evil, definitely challenged and resolutely subdued, there is no trace in his conceptions of young men. Whereas in his imaginations of women, —in the characters of Ellen Douglas, of Flora MacIvor, Rose Bradwardine, Catherine Seyton, Diana Vernon, Lilias Redgauntlet, Alice Bridgenorth, Alice Lee, and Jeanie Deans, —with endless varieties of grace, tenderness, and intellectual power, we find in all a quite infallible sense of dignity and justice; a fearless, instant, and untiring self-sacrifice, to even the appearance of duty, much more to its real claims; and, finally, a patient wisdom of deeply-restrained affection, which does infinitely more than protect its objects from a momentary error; it gradually forms, animates, and exalts the characters of the unworthy lovers, until, at the close of the tale, we are just able, and no more, to take patience in hearing of their unmerited success.

So that, in all cases, with Scott as with Shakespeare, it is the woman who watches over, teaches, and guides the youth; it is never, by any chance, the youth who watches over, or educates, his mistress.

Next take, though more briefly, graver testimony—that of the great Italians and Greeks. You know well the plan of Dante's great poem— that it is a love-poem to his dead lady; a song of praise for her watch over his soul. Stooping only to pity, never to love, she yet saves him from destruction—saves him from hell. He is going eternally astray in despair; she comes down from heaven to his help, and throughout the ascents of Paradise is his teacher, interpreting for him the most difficult truths, divine and human; and leading him, with rebuke upon rebuke, from star to star.

I do not insist upon Dante's conception; if I began I could not cease: besides, you might think this a wild imagination of one poet's heart. So I will rather read to you a few verses of the deliberate writing of a knight of Pisa to his living lady, wholly characteristic of the feeling of all the noblest men of the thirteenth, or early fourteenth, century, preserved among many other such records of knightly honour and love, which Dante Rossetti has gathered for us from among the early Italian poets.

"For lo! thy law is passed
That this my love should manifestly be
To serve and honour thee:
And so I do; and my delight is full,
Accepted for the servant of thy rule.

"Without almost, I am all rapturous,
Since thus my will was set
To serve, thou flower of joy, thine excellence:
Nor ever seems it anything could rouse
A pain or a regret.

But on thee dwells my every thought and sense;
Considering that from thee all virtues spread
As from a fountain head,—
THAT IN THY GIFT IS WISDOM'S BEST AVAIL,

AND HONOUR WITHOUT FAIL,
With whom each sovereign good dwells separate,
Fulfilling the perfection of thy state.

"Lady, since I conceived
Thy pleasurable aspect in my heart,
MY LIFE HAS BEEN APART
IN SHINING BRIGHTNESS AND THE PLACE OF TRUTH;
Which till that time, good sooth,
Groped among shadows in a darken'd place,
Where many hours and days
It hardly ever had remember'd good.
But now my servitude
Is thine, and I am full of joy and rest.
A man from a wild beast
Thou madest me, since for thy love I lived."

You may think perhaps a Greek knight would have had a lower estimate of women than this Christian lover. His spiritual subjection to them was indeed not so absolute; but as regards their own personal character, it was only because you could not have followed me so easily, that I did not take the Greek women instead of Shakespeare's; and instance, for chief ideal types of human beauty and faith, the simple mother's and wife's heart of Andromache; the divine, yet rejected wisdom of Cassandra; the playful kindness and simple princess-life of happy Nausicaa; the housewifely calm of that of Penelope, with its watch upon the sea; the ever patient, fearless, hopelessly devoted piety of the sister, and daughter, in Antigone; the bowing down of Iphigenia, lamb-like and silent; and finally, the expectation of the resurrection, made clear to the soul of the Greeks in the return from her grave of that Alcestis, who, to save her husband, had passed calmly through the bitterness of death.

Now I could multiply witness upon witness of this kind upon you if I had time. I would take Chaucer, and show you why he wrote a Legend of Good Women; but no Legend of Good Men. I would take Spenser, and show you how all his fairy knights are sometimes deceived and sometimes vanquished; but the soul of Una is never darkened, and the spear of Britomart is never broken. Nay, I could go back into the mythical teaching of the most ancient times, and show you how the great people, —by one of whose princesses it was appointed that the Lawgiver of all the earth should be educated, rather than by his own kindred; —how that great Egyptian people, wisest then of nations, gave to their Spirit of Wisdom the form of a Woman; and into her hand, for a symbol, the weaver's shuttle; and how the name and the form of that spirit, adopted, believed, and obeyed by the Greeks, became that Athena of the olive-helm, and cloudy shield, to faith in whom you owe, down to this date, whatever you hold most precious in art, in literature, or in types of national virtue.

But I will not wander into this distant and mythical element; I will only ask you to give its legitimate value to the testimony of these great poets and men of the world, —consistent, as you see it is, on this head. I will ask you whether it can be supposed that these men, in the main work of their lives, are amusing themselves with a fictitious and idle view of the relations between man and woman; — nay, worse than fictitious or idle; for a thing may be imaginary, yet desirable, if it were possible: but this, their ideal of woman, is, according to our common idea of the marriage relation, wholly undesirable. The woman, we say, is not to guide, nor even to think for herself. The man is always to be the wiser; he is to be the thinker, the ruler, the superior in knowledge and discretion, as in power.

Is it not somewhat important to make up our minds on this matter? Are all these great men mistaken, or are we? Are Shakespeare and AEschylus, Dante and Homer, merely dressing dolls for us; or, worse than dolls, unnatural visions, the realization of which, were it possible, would bring anarchy into all households and ruin into all affections? Nay, if you can suppose this, take lastly the evidence of facts, given by the human heart itself. In all Christian ages which have been remarkable for their purity or progress, there has been absolute yielding of obedient devotion, by the lover, to his mistress. I say OBEDIENT; —not merely enthusiastic and worshipping in imagination, but entirely subject, receiving from the beloved woman, however young, not only the encouragement, the praise, and the reward of all toil, but, so far as any choice is open, or any question difficult of decision, the DIRECTION of all toil. That chivalry, to the abuse and dishonour of which are attributable primarily whatever is cruel in war, unjust in peace, or corrupt and ignoble in domestic relations; and to the original purity and power of which we owe the defence alike of faith, of law, and of love; that chivalry, I say, in its very first conception of honourable life, assumes the subjection of the young knight to the command— should it even be the command in caprice—of his lady. It assumes this, because its masters knew that the first and necessary impulse of every truly taught and knightly heart is this of blind service to its lady: that where that true faith and captivity are not, all wayward and wicked passion must be; and that in this rapturous obedience to the single love of his youth, is the sanctification of all man's strength, and the continuance of all his purposes. And this, not because such obedience would be safe, or honourable, were it ever rendered to the unworthy; but because it ought to be impossible for every noble youth—it IS impossible for every one rightly trained—to love any one whose gentle counsel he cannot trust, or whose prayerful command he can hesitate to obey.

I do not insist by any farther argument on this, for I think it should commend itself at once to your knowledge of what has been and to your feeling of what should be. You cannot think that the buckling on of the knight's armour by his lady's hand was a mere caprice of romantic fashion. It is the type of an eternal truth— that the soul's armour is never well set to the heart unless a woman's hand has braced it; and it is only when she braces it loosely that the honour of manhood fails. Know you not those lovely lines—I would they were learned by all youthful ladies of England: -

"Ah, wasteful woman!—she who may
On her sweet self set her own price,
Knowing he cannot choose but pay -
How has she cheapen'd Paradise!
How given for nought her priceless gift,
How spoiled the bread and spill'd the wine,
Which, spent with due respective thrift,
Had made brutes men, and men divine!" {24}

Thus much, then, respecting the relations of lovers I believe you will accept. But what we too often doubt is the fitness of the continuance of such a relation throughout the whole of human life. We think it right in the lover and mistress, not in the husband and wife. That is to say, we think that a reverent and tender duty is due to one whose affection we still doubt, and whose character we as yet do but partially and distantly discern; and that this reverence and duty are to be withdrawn when the affection has become wholly and limitlessly our own, and the character has been so sifted and tried that we fear not to entrust it with the happiness of our lives. Do you not see how ignoble this is, as well as how unreasonable? Do you not feel that marriage, —when it is marriage at all, —is only the seal which marks the vowed transition of temporary into untiring service, and of fitful into eternal love?

But how, you will ask, is the idea of this guiding function of the woman reconcilable with a true wifely subjection? Simply in that it is a GUIDING, not a determining, function. Let me try to show you briefly how these powers seem to be rightly distinguishable.

We are foolish, and without excuse foolish, in speaking of the "superiority" of one sex to the other, as if they could be compared in similar things. Each has what the other has not: each completes the other, and is completed by the other: they are in nothing alike, and the happiness and perfection of both depends on each asking and receiving from the other what the other only can give.

Now their separate characters are briefly these. The man's power is active, progressive, defensive. He is eminently the doer, the creator, the discoverer, the defender. His intellect is for speculation and invention; his energy for adventure, for war, and for conquest, wherever war is just, wherever conquest necessary. But the woman's power is for rule, not for battle, —and her intellect is not for invention or creation, but for sweet ordering, arrangement, and decision. She sees the qualities of things, their claims, and their places. Her great function is Praise; she enters into no contest, but infallibly adjudges the crown of contest. By her office, and place, she is protected from all danger and temptation. The man, in his rough work in open world, must encounter all peril and trial; —to him, therefore, must be the failure, the offence, the inevitable error: often he must be wounded, or subdued; often misled; and ALWAYS hardened. But he guards the woman from all this; within his house, as ruled by her, unless she herself has sought it, need enter no danger, no temptation, no cause of error or offence. This is the true nature of home—it is the place of Peace; the shelter, not only from all injury, but from all terror, doubt, and division. In so far as it is not this, it is not home; so far as the anxieties of the outer life penetrate into it, and the inconsistently-minded, unknown, unloved, or hostile society of the outer world is allowed by either husband or wife to cross the threshold, it ceases to be home; it is then only a part of that outer world which you have roofed over, and lighted fire in. But so far as it is a sacred place, a vestal temple, a temple of the hearth watched over by Household Gods, before whose faces none may come but those whom they can receive with love, —so far as it is this, and roof and fire are types only of a nobler shade and light, —shade as of the rock in a weary land, and light as of the Pharos in the stormy sea; —so far it vindicates the name, and fulfils the praise, of Home.

And wherever a true wife comes, this home is always round her. The stars only may be over her head; the glowworm in the night-cold grass may be the only fire at her foot; but home is yet wherever she is; and for a noble woman it stretches far round her, better than ceiled with cedar, or painted with vermilion, shedding its quiet light far, for those who else were homeless.

This, then, I believe to be, —will you not admit it to be, —the woman's true place and power? But do not you see that, to fulfil this, she must—as far as one can use such terms of a human creature—be incapable of error? So far as she rules, all must be right, or nothing is. She must be enduringly, incorruptibly good; instinctively, infallibly wise—wise, not for self-development, but for self-renunciation: wise, not that she may set herself above her husband, but that she may never fail from his side: wise, not with the narrowness of insolent and loveless pride, but with the passionate gentleness of an infinitely variable, because infinitely applicable, modesty of service—the true changefulness of woman. In that great sense—"La donna e mobile, " not "Qual pium' al vento"; no, nor yet "Variable as the shade, by the light quivering aspen made"; but variable as the LIGHT, manifold in fair and serene division, that it may take the colour of all that it falls upon, and exalt it.

(II.) I have been trying, thus far, to show you what should be the place, and what the power of woman. Now, secondly, we ask, What kind of education is to fit her for these?

And if you indeed think this a true conception of her office and dignity, it will not be difficult to trace the course of education which would fit her for the one, and raise her to the other.

The first of our duties to her—no thoughtful persons now doubt this, —is to secure for her such physical training and exercise as may confirm her health, and perfect her beauty; the highest refinement of that beauty being unattainable without splendour of activity and of delicate strength. To perfect her beauty, I say, and increase its power; it cannot be too powerful, nor shed its sacred light too far: only remember that all physical freedom is vain to produce beauty without a corresponding freedom of heart. There are two passages of that poet who is distinguished, it seems to me, from all others—not by power, but by exquisite RIGHTNESS— which point you to the source, and describe to you, in a few syllables, the completion of womanly beauty. I will read the introductory stanzas, but the last is the one I wish you specially to notice: -

"Three years she grew in sun and shower,
Then Nature said, 'A lovelier flower
On earth was never sown;
This child I to myself will take;
She shall be mine, and I will make
A lady of my own.'

'Myself will to my darling be
Both law and impulse; and with me
The girl, in rock and plain,
In earth and heaven, in glade and bower,
Shall feel an overseeing power
To kindle, or restrain.'

'The floating clouds their state shall lend
To her, for her the willow bend;
Nor shall she fail to see,
Even in the motions of the storm,
Grace that shall mould the maiden's form
By silent sympathy.'

'And VITAL FEELINGS OF DELIGHT
Shall rear her form to stately height, -
Her virgin bosom swell.
Such thoughts to Lucy I will give,
While she and I together live,
Here in this happy dell.'" {25}

"VITAL feelings of delight, " observe. There are deadly feelings of delight; but the natural ones are vital, necessary to very life.

And they must be feelings of delight, if they are to be vital. Do not think you can make a girl lovely, if you do not make her happy. There is not one restraint you put on a good girl's nature—there is not one check you give to her instincts of affection or of effort—which will not be indelibly written on her features, with a hardness which is all the more painful because it takes away the brightness from the eyes of innocence, and the charm from the brow of virtue.

This for the means: now note the end.

Take from the same poet, in two lines, a perfect description of womanly beauty -

"A countenance in which did meet
Sweet records, promises as sweet."

The perfect loveliness of a woman's countenance can only consist in that majestic peace, which is founded in the memory of happy and useful years, —full of sweet records; and from the joining of this with that yet more majestic childishness, which is still full of change and promise; —opening always—modest at once, and bright, with hope of better things to be won, and to be bestowed. There is no old age where there is still that promise.

Thus, then, you have first to mould her physical frame, and then, as the strength she gains will permit you, to fill and temper her mind with all knowledge and thoughts which tend to confirm its natural instincts of justice, and refine its natural tact of love.

All such knowledge should be given her as may enable her to understand, and even to aid, the work of men: and yet it should be given, not as knowledge, —not as if it were, or could be, for her an object to know; but only to feel, and to judge. It is of no moment, as a matter of pride or perfectness in herself, whether she knows many languages or one; but it is of the utmost, that she should be able to show kindness to a stranger, and to understand the sweetness of a stranger's tongue. It is of no moment to her own worth or dignity that she should be acquainted with this science or that; but it is of the highest that she should be trained in habits of accurate thought; that she should understand the meaning, the inevitableness, and the loveliness of natural laws; and follow at least some one path of scientific attainment, as far as to the threshold of that bitter Valley of Humiliation, into which only the wisest and bravest of men can descend, owning themselves for ever children, gathering pebbles on a boundless shore. It is of little consequence how many positions of cities she knows, or how many dates of events, or names of celebrated persons—it is not the object of education to turn the woman into a dictionary; but it is deeply necessary that she should be taught to enter with her whole personality into the history she reads; to picture the passages of it vitally in her own bright imagination; to apprehend, with her fine instincts, the pathetic circumstances and dramatic relations, which the historian too often only eclipses by his reasoning, and disconnects by his arrangement:

it is for her to trace the hidden equities of divine reward, and catch sight, through the darkness, of the fateful threads of woven fire that connect error with retribution. But, chiefly of all, she is to be taught to extend the limits of her sympathy with respect to that history which is being for ever determined as the moments pass in which she draws her peaceful breath; and to the contemporary calamity, which, were it but rightly mourned by her, would recur no more hereafter. She is to exercise herself in imagining what would be the effects upon her mind and conduct, if she were daily brought into the presence of the suffering which is not the less real because shut from her sight. She is to be taught somewhat to understand the nothingness of the proportion which that little world in which she lives and loves, bears to the world in which God lives and loves; —and solemnly she is to be taught to strive that her thoughts of piety may not be feeble in proportion to the number they embrace, nor her prayer more languid than it is for the momentary relief from pain of her husband or her child, when it is uttered for the multitudes of those who have none to love them, —and is "for all who are desolate and oppressed. "

Thus far, I think, I have had your concurrence; perhaps you will not be with me in what I believe is most needful for me to say. There IS one dangerous science for women—one which they must indeed beware how they profanely touch—that of theology. Strange, and miserably strange, that while they are modest enough to doubt their powers, and pause at the threshold of sciences where every step is demonstrable and sure, they will plunge headlong, and without one thought of incompetency, into that science in which the greatest men have trembled, and the wisest erred. Strange, that they will complacently and pridefully bind up whatever vice or folly there is in them, whatever arrogance, petulance, or blind incomprehensiveness, into one bitter bundle of consecrated myrrh. Strange, in creatures born to be Love visible, that where they can know least, they will condemn, first, and think to recommend themselves to their Master, by crawling up the steps of His judgment-throne to divide it with Him. Strangest of all that they should think they were led by the Spirit of the Comforter into habits of mind which have become in them the unmixed elements of home discomfort; and that they dare to turn the Household Gods of Christianity into ugly idols of their own; —spiritual dolls, for them to dress according to their caprice; and from which their husbands must turn away in grieved contempt, lest they should be shrieked at for breaking them.

I believe, then, with this exception, that a girl's education should be nearly, in its course and material of study, the same as a boy's; but quite differently directed. A woman, in any rank of life, ought to know whatever her husband is likely to know, but to know it in a different way. His command of it should be foundational and progressive; hers, general and accomplished for daily and helpful use. Not but that it would often be wiser in men to learn things in a womanly sort of way, for present use, and to seek for the discipline and training of their mental powers in such branches of study as will be afterwards fittest for social service; but, speaking broadly, a man ought to know any language or science he learns, thoroughly—while a woman ought to know the same language, or science, only so far as may enable her to sympathise in her husband's pleasures, and in those of his best friends.

Yet, observe, with exquisite accuracy as far as she reaches. There is a wide difference between elementary knowledge and superficial knowledge—between a firm beginning, and an infirm attempt at compassing. A woman may always help her husband by what she knows, however little; by what she half-knows, or mis-knows, she will only tease him.

And indeed, if there were to be any difference between a girl's education and a boy's, I should say that of the two the girl should be earlier led, as her intellect ripens faster, into deep and serious subjects: and that her range of literature should be, not more, but less frivolous; calculated to add the qualities of patience and seriousness to her natural poignancy of thought and quickness of wit; and also to keep her in a lofty and pure element of thought. I enter not now into any question of choice of books; only let us be sure that her books are not heaped up in her lap as they fall out of the package of the circulating library, wet with the last and lightest spray of the fountain of folly.

Or even of the fountain of wit; for with respect to the sore temptation of novel reading, it is not the badness of a novel that we should dread, so much as its over-wrought interest. The weakest romance is not so stupefying as the lower forms of religious exciting literature, and the worst romance is not so corrupting as false history, false philosophy, or false political essays. But the best romance becomes dangerous, if, by its excitement, it renders the ordinary course of life uninteresting, and increases the morbid thirst for useless acquaintance with scenes in which we shall never be called upon to act.

I speak therefore of good novels only; and our modern literature is particularly rich in types of such. Well read, indeed, these books have serious use, being nothing less than treatises on moral anatomy and chemistry; studies of human nature in the elements of it. But I attach little weight to this function: they are hardly ever read with earnestness enough to permit them to fulfil it. The utmost they usually do is to enlarge somewhat the charity of a kind reader, or the bitterness of a malicious one; for each will gather, from the novel, food for her own disposition. Those who are naturally proud and envious will learn from Thackeray to despise humanity; those who are naturally gentle, to pity it; those who are naturally shallow, to laugh at it. So, also, there might be a serviceable power in novels to bring before us, in vividness, a human truth which we had before dimly conceived; but the temptation to picturesqueness of statement is so great, that often the best writers of fiction cannot resist it; and our views are rendered so violent and one-sided, that their vitality is rather a harm than good.

Without, however, venturing here on any attempt at decision how much novel reading should be allowed, let me at least clearly assert this, —that whether novels, or poetry, or history be read, they should be chosen, not for their freedom from evil, but for their possession of good. The chance and scattered evil that may here and there haunt, or hide itself in, a powerful book, never does any harm to a noble girl; but the emptiness of an author oppresses her, and his amiable folly degrades her. And if she can have access to a good library of old and classical books, there need be no choosing at all. Keep the modern magazine and novel out of your girl's way: turn her loose into the old library every wet day, and let her alone. She will find what is good for her; you cannot: for there is just this difference between the making of a girl's character and a boy's—you may chisel a boy into shape, as you would a rock, or hammer him into it, if he be of a better kind, as you would a piece of bronze. But you cannot hammer a girl into anything. She grows as a flower does, —she will wither without sun; she will decay in her sheath, as a narcissus will, if you do not give her air enough; she may fall, and defile her head in dust, if you leave her without help at some moments of her life; but you cannot fetter her; she must take her own fair form and way, if she take any, and in mind as in body, must have always

"Her household motions light and free
And steps of virgin liberty. "

Let her loose in the library, I say, as you do a fawn in a field. It knows the bad weeds twenty times better than you; and the good ones too, and will eat some bitter and prickly ones, good for it, which you had not the slightest thought would have been so.

Then, in art, keep the finest models before her, and let her practice in all accomplishments be accurate and thorough, so as to enable her to understand more than she accomplishes. I say the finest models—that is to say, the truest, simplest, usefullest. Note those epithets: they will range through all the arts. Try them in music, where you might think them the least applicable. I say the truest, that in which the notes most closely and faithfully express the meaning of the words, or the character of intended emotion; again, the simplest, that in which the meaning and melody are attained with the fewest and most significant notes possible; and, finally, the usefullest, that music which makes the best words most beautiful, which enchants them in our memories each with its own glory of sound, and which applies them closest to the heart at the moment we need them.

And not only in the material and in the course, but yet more earnestly in the spirit of it, let a girl's education be as serious as a boy's. You bring up your girls as if they were meant for sideboard ornaments, and then complain of their frivolity. Give them the same advantages that you give their brothers—appeal to the same grand instincts of virtue in them; teach THEM, also, that courage and truth are the pillars of their being: - do you think that they would not answer that appeal, brave and true as they are even now, when you know that there is hardly a girls' school in this Christian kingdom where the children's courage or sincerity would be thought of half so much importance as their way of coming in at a door; and when the whole system of society, as respects the mode of establishing them in life, is one rotten plague of cowardice and imposture—cowardice, in not daring to let them live, or love, except as their neighbours choose; and imposture, in bringing, for the purposes of our own pride, the full glow of the world's worst vanity upon a girl's eyes, at the very period when the whole happiness of her future existence depends upon her remaining undazzled?

And give them, lastly, not only noble teachings, but noble teachers. You consider somewhat before you send your boy to school, what kind of a man the master is; —whatsoever kind of a man he is, you at least give him full authority over your son, and show some respect to him yourself; —if he comes to dine with you, you do not put him at a side table: you know also that, at college, your child's immediate tutor will be under the direction of some still higher tutor, —for whom you have absolute reverence. You do not treat the Dean of Christ Church or the Master of Trinity as your inferiors.

But what teachers do you give your girls, and what reverence do you show to the teachers you have chosen? Is a girl likely to think her own conduct, or her own intellect, of much importance, when you trust the entire formation of her character, moral and intellectual, to a person whom you let your servants treat with less respect than they do your housekeeper (as if the soul of your child were a less charge than jams and groceries), and whom you yourself think you confer an honour upon by letting her sometimes sit in the drawing-room in the evening?

Thus, then, of literature as her help, and thus of art. There is one more help which she cannot do without—one which, alone, has sometimes done more than all other influences besides, —the help of wild and fair nature. Hear this of the education of Joan of Arc: -

"The education of this poor girl was mean, according to the present standard; was ineffably grand, according to a purer philosophic standard; and only not good for our age, because for us it would be unattainable.

" Next after her spiritual advantages, she owed most to the advantages of her situation. The fountain of Domremy was on the brink of a boundless forest; and it was haunted to that degree by fairies, that the parish priest (cure) was obliged to read mass there once a year, in order to keep them in decent bounds.

"But the forests of Domremy—those were the glories of the land; for in them abode mysterious powers and ancient secrets that towered into tragic strength. Abbeys there were, and abbey windows, —'like Moorish temples of the Hindoos, ' that exercised even princely power both in Touraine and in the German Diets. These had their sweet bells that pierced the forests for many a league at matins or vespers, and each its own dreamy legend. Few enough, and scattered enough, were these abbeys, so as in no degree to disturb the deep solitude of the region; yet many enough to spread a network or awning of Christian sanctity over what else might have seemed a heathen wilderness. " {26}

Now, you cannot, indeed, have here in England, woods eighteen miles deep to the centre; but you can, perhaps, keep a fairy or two for your children yet, if you wish to keep them. But DO you wish it? Suppose you had each, at the back of your houses, a garden, large enough for your children to play in, with just as much lawn as would give them room to run, —no more—and that you could not change your abode; but that, if you chose, you could double your income, or quadruple it, by digging a coal shaft in the middle of the lawn, and turning the flower-beds into heaps of coke. Would you do it? I hope not. I can tell you, you would be wrong if you did, though it gave you income sixty-fold instead of four-fold.

Yet this is what you are doing with all England. The whole country is but a little garden, not more than enough for your children to run on the lawns of, if you would let them all run there. And this little garden you will turn into furnace ground, and fill with heaps of cinders, if you can; and those children of yours, not you, will suffer for it. For the fairies will not be all banished; there are fairies of the furnace as of the wood, and their first gifts seem to be "sharp arrows of the mighty; " but their last gifts are "coals of juniper. "

And yet I cannot—though there is no part of my subject that I feel more—press this upon you; for we made so little use of the power of nature while we had it that we shall hardly feel what we have lost. Just on the other side of the Mersey you have your Snowdon, and your Menai Straits, and that mighty granite rock beyond the moors of Anglesea, splendid in its heathery crest, and foot planted in the deep sea, once thought of as sacred—a divine promontory, looking westward; the Holy Head or Headland, still not without awe when its red light glares first through storm. These are the hills, and these the bays and blue inlets, which, among the Greeks, would have been always loved, always fateful in influence on the national mind. That Snowdon is your Parnassus; but where are its Muses? That Holyhead mountain is your Island of AEgina; but where is its Temple to Minerva?

Shall I read you what the Christian Minerva had achieved under the shadow of our Parnassus up to the year 1848? —Here is a little account of a Welsh school, from page 261 of the Report on Wales, published by the Committee of Council on Education. This is a school close to a town containing 5,000 persons: -

"I then called up a larger class, most of whom had recently come to the school. Three girls repeatedly declared they had never heard of Christ, and two that they had never heard of God. Two out of six thought Christ was on earth now" (they might have had a worse thought perhaps), "three knew nothing about the Crucifixion. Four out of seven did not know the names of the months nor the number of days in a year. They had no notion of addition beyond two and two, or three and three; their minds were perfect blanks. "

Oh, ye women of England! from the Princess of that Wales to the simplest of you, do not think your own children can be brought into their true fold of rest, while these are scattered on the hills, as sheep having no shepherd. And do not think your daughters can be trained to the truth of their own human beauty, while the pleasant places, which God made at once for their schoolroom and their playground, lie desolate and defiled. You cannot baptize them rightly in those inch-deep fonts of yours, unless you baptize them also in the sweet waters which the great Lawgiver strikes forth for ever from the rocks of your native land—waters which a Pagan would have worshipped in their purity, and you worship only with pollution. You cannot lead your children faithfully to those narrow axe-hewn church altars of yours, while the dark azure altars in heaven—the mountains that sustain your island throne, —mountains on which a Pagan would have seen the powers of heaven rest in every wreathed cloud—remain for you without inscription; altars built, not to, but by an Unknown God.

(III.) Thus far, then, of the nature, thus far of the teaching, of woman, and thus of her household office, and queenliness. We now come to our last, our widest question. —What is her queenly office with respect to the state?

Generally, we are under an impression that a man's duties are public, and a woman's private. But this is not altogether so. A man has a personal work or duty, relating to his own home, and a public work or duty, which is the expansion of the other, relating to the state. So a woman has a personal work or duty, relating to her own home, and a public work or duty, which is also the expansion of that.

Now the man's work for his own home is, as has been said, to secure its maintenance, progress, and defence; the woman's to secure its order, comfort, and loveliness.

Expand both these functions. The man's duty as a member of a commonwealth, is to assist in the maintenance, in the advance, in the defence of the state. The woman's duty, as a member of the commonwealth, is to assist in the ordering, in the comforting, and in the beautiful adornment of the state.

What the man is at his own gate, defending it, if need be, against insult and spoil, that also, not in a less, but in a more devoted measure, he is to be at the gate of his country, leaving his home, if need be, even to the spoiler, to do his more incumbent work there.

And, in like manner, what the woman is to be within her gates, as the centre of order, the balm of distress, and the mirror of beauty: that she is also to be without her gates, where order is more difficult, distress more imminent, loveliness more rare.

And as within the human heart there is always set an instinct for all its real duties, —an instinct which you cannot quench, but only warp and corrupt if you withdraw it from its true purpose: - as there is the intense instinct of love, which, rightly disciplined, maintains all the sanctities of life, and, misdirected, undermines them; and MUST do either the one or the other; —so there is in the human heart an inextinguishable instinct, the love of power, which, rightly directed, maintains all the majesty of law and life, and, misdirected, wrecks them.

Deep rooted in the innermost life of the heart of man, and of the heart of woman, God set it there, and God keeps it there. —Vainly, as falsely, you blame or rebuke the desire of power! —For Heaven's sake, and for Man's sake, desire it all you can. But WHAT power? That is all the question. Power to destroy? the lion's limb, and the dragon's breath? Not so. Power to heal, to redeem, to guide, and to guard. Power of the sceptre and shield; the power of the royal hand that heals in touching, —that binds the fiend, and looses the captive; the throne that is founded on the rock of Justice, and descended from only by steps of Mercy. Will you not covet such power as this, and seek such throne as this, and be no more housewives, but queens?

It is now long since the women of England arrogated, universally, a title which once belonged to nobility only; and, having once been in the habit of accepting the simple title of gentlewoman as correspondent to that of gentleman, insisted on the privilege of assuming the title of "Lady, " {27} which properly corresponds only to the title of "Lord. "

I do not blame them for this; but only for their narrow motive in this. I would have them desire and claim the title of Lady, provided they claim, not merely the title, but the office and duty signified by it. Lady means "bread-giver" or "loaf-giver, " and Lord means "maintainer of laws, " and both titles have reference, not to the law which is maintained in the house, nor to the bread which is given to the household; but to law maintained for the multitude, and to bread broken among the multitude. So that a Lord has legal claim only to his title in so far as he is the maintainer of the justice of the Lord of lords; and a Lady has legal claim to her title only so far as she communicates that help to the poor representatives of her Master, which women once, ministering to Him of their substance, were permitted to extend to that Master Himself; and when she is known, as He Himself once was, in breaking of bread.

And this beneficent and legal dominion, this power of the Dominus, or House-Lord, and of the Domina, or House-Lady, is great and venerable, not in the number of those through whom it has lineally descended, but in the number of those whom it grasps within its sway; it is always regarded with reverent worship wherever its dynasty is founded on its duty, and its ambition correlative with its beneficence. Your fancy is pleased with the thought of being noble ladies, with a train of vassals. Be it so; you cannot be too noble, and your train cannot be too great; but see to it that your train is of vassals whom you serve and feed, not merely of slaves who serve and feed you; and that the multitude which obeys you is of those whom you have comforted, not oppressed, —whom you have redeemed, not led into captivity.

And this, which is true of the lower or household dominion, is equally true of the queenly dominion; that highest dignity is open to you, if you will also accept that highest duty. Rex et Regina— Roi et Reine—"RIGHT-doers; " they differ but from the Lady and Lord, in that their power is supreme over the mind as over the person— that they not only feed and clothe, but direct and teach. And whether consciously or not, you must be, in many a heart, enthroned: there is no putting by that crown; queens you must always be: queens to your lovers; queens to your husbands and your sons; queens of higher mystery to the world beyond, which bows itself, and will for ever bow, before the myrtle crown and the stainless sceptre of womanhood. But, alas! you are too often idle and careless queens, grasping at majesty in the least things, while you abdicate it in the greatest; and leaving misrule and violence to work their will among men, in defiance of the power which, holding straight in gift from the Prince of all Peace, the wicked among you betray, and the good forget.

"Prince of Peace. " Note that name. When kings rule in that name, and nobles, and the judges of the earth, they also, in their narrow place, and mortal measure, receive the power of it. There are no other rulers than they; other rule than theirs is but MISrule; they who govern verily "Dei Gratia" are all princes, yes, or princesses of Peace. There is not a war in the world, no, nor an injustice, but you women are answerable for it; not in that you have provoked, but in that you have not hindered. Men, by their nature, are prone to fight; they will fight for any cause, or for none. It is for you to choose their cause for them, and to forbid them when there is no cause. There is no suffering, no injustice, no misery, in the earth, but the guilt of it lies with you. Men can bear the sight of it, but you should not be able to bear it. Men may tread it down without sympathy in their own struggle; but men are feeble in sympathy, and contracted in hope; it is you only who can feel the depths of pain, and conceive the way of its healing. Instead of trying to do this, you turn away from it; you shut yourselves within your park walls and garden gates; and you are content to know that there is beyond them a whole world in wilderness—a world of secrets which you dare not penetrate; and of suffering which you dare not conceive.

I tell you that this is to me quite the most amazing among the phenomena of humanity. I am surprised at no depths to which, when once warped from its honour, that humanity can be degraded. I do not wonder at the miser's death, with his hands, as they relax, dropping gold. I do not wonder at the sensualist's life, with the shroud wrapped about his feet. I do not wonder at the single-handed murder of a single victim, done by the assassin in the darkness of the railway, or reed shadow of the marsh. I do not even wonder at the myriad-handed murder of multitudes, done boastfully in the daylight, by the frenzy of nations, and the immeasurable, unimaginable guilt heaped up from hell to heaven, of their priests, and kings. But this is wonderful to me—oh, how wonderful! —to see the tender and delicate woman among you, with her child at her breast, and a power, if she would wield it, over it, and over its father, purer than the air of heaven, and stronger than the seas of earth—nay, a magnitude of blessing which her husband would not part with for all that earth itself, though it were made of one entire and perfect chrysolite: - to see her abdicate this majesty to play at precedence with her next-door neighbour! This is wonderful—oh, wonderful! —to see her, with every innocent feeling fresh within her, go out in the morning into her garden to play with the fringes of its guarded flowers, and lift their heads when they are drooping, with her happy smile upon her face, and no cloud upon her brow, because there is a little wall around her place of peace: and yet she knows, in her heart, if she would only look for its knowledge, that, outside of that little rose-covered wall, the wild grass, to the horizon, is torn up by the agony of men, and beat level by the drift of their life-blood.

Have you ever considered what a deep under meaning there lies, or at least may be read, if we choose, in our custom of strewing flowers before those whom we think most happy? Do you suppose it is merely to deceive them into the hope that happiness is always to fall thus in showers at their feet? —that wherever they pass they will tread on herbs of sweet scent, and that the rough ground will be made smooth for them by depths of roses? So surely as they believe that, they will have, instead, to walk on bitter herbs and thorns; and the only softness to their feet will be of snow. But it is not thus intended they should believe; there is a better meaning in that old custom. The path of a good woman is indeed strewn with flowers; but they rise behind her steps, not before them. "Her feet have touched the meadows, and left the daisies rosy. "

You think that only a lover's fancy; —false and vain! How if it could be true? You think this also, perhaps, only a poet's fancy -

> "Even the light harebell raised its head
> Elastic from her airy tread."

But it is little to say of a woman, that she only does not destroy where she passes. She should revive; the harebells should bloom, not stoop, as she passes. You think I am rushing into wild hyperbole! Pardon me, not a whit—I mean what I say in calm English, spoken in resolute truth. You have heard it said—(and I believe there is more than fancy even in that saying, but let it pass for a fanciful one)—that flowers only flourish rightly in the garden of some one who loves them. I know you would like that to be true; you would think it a pleasant magic if you could flush your flowers into brighter bloom by a kind look upon them: nay, more, if your look had the power, not only to cheer, but to guard; —if you could bid the black blight turn away, and the knotted caterpillar spare—if you could bid the dew fall upon them in the drought, and say to the south wind, in frost—"Come, thou south, and breathe upon my garden, that the spices of it may flow out. " This you would think a great thing? And do you think it not a greater thing, that all this, (and how much more than this!) you CAN do, for fairer flowers than these—flowers that could bless you for having blessed them, and will love you for having loved them; flowers that have thoughts like yours, and lives like yours; and which, once saved, you save for ever? Is this only a little power? Far among the moorlands and the rocks, —far in the darkness of the terrible streets, —these feeble florets are lying, with all their fresh leaves torn, and their stems broken: will you never go down to them, nor set them in order in their little fragrant beds, nor fence them in their trembling, from the fierce wind? Shall morning follow morning, for you, but not for them; and the dawn rise to watch, far away, those frantic Dances of Death; {28} but no dawn rise to breathe upon these living banks of wild violet, and woodbine, and rose; nor call to you, through your casement—call (not giving you the name of the English poet's lady, but the name of Dante's great Matilda, who, on the edge of happy Lethe, stood, wreathing flowers with flowers), saying: -

"Come into the garden, Maud,
For the black bat, night, has flown,
And the woodbine spices are wafted abroad,
And the musk of the roses blown"?

Will you not go down among them? —among those sweet living things, whose new courage, sprung from the earth with the deep colour of heaven upon it, is starting up in strength of goodly spire; and whose purity, washed from the dust, is opening, bud by bud, into the flower of promise; —and still they turn to you, and for you, "The Larkspur listens—I hear, I hear! And the Lily whispers—I wait."

Did you notice that I missed two lines when I read you that first stanza; and think that I had forgotten them? Hear them now: -

"Come into the garden, Maud,
For the black bat, night, has flown,
Come into the garden, Maud,
I am here at the gate, alone."

Who is it, think you, who stands at the gate of this sweeter garden alone, waiting for you? Did you ever hear, not of a Maud, but a Madeleine, who went down to her garden in the dawn, and found One waiting at the gate, whom she supposed to be the gardener? Have you not sought Him often; —sought Him in vain, all through the night; — sought Him in vain at the gate of that old garden where the fiery sword is set? He is never there; but at the gate of THIS garden He is waiting always—waiting to take your hand—ready to go down to see the fruits of the valley, to see whether the vine has flourished, and the pomegranate budded. There you shall see with Him the little tendrils of the vines that His hand is guiding—there you shall see the pomegranate springing where His hand cast the sanguine seed; —more: you shall see the troops of the angel keepers that, with their wings, wave away the hungry birds from the path-sides where He has sown, and call to each other between the vineyard rows, "Take us the foxes, the little foxes, that spoil the vines, for our vines have tender grapes. " Oh—you queens—you queens! among the hills and happy greenwood of this land of yours, shall the foxes have holes, and the birds of the air have nests; and in your cities, shall the stones cry out against you, that they are the only pillows where the Son of Man can lay His head?

PREFACE TO THE LATER EDITIONS

Being now fifty-one years old, and little likely to change my mind hereafter on any important subject of thought (unless through weakness of age), I wish to publish a connected series of such parts of my works as now seem to me right, and likely to be of permanent use. In doing so I shall omit much, but not attempt to mend what I think worth reprinting. A young man necessarily writes otherwise than an old one, and it would be worse than wasted time to try to recast the juvenile language: nor is it to be thought that I am ashamed even of what I cancel; for great part of my earlier work was rapidly written for temporary purposes, and is now unnecessary, though true, even to truism. What I wrote about religion, was, on the contrary, painstaking, and, I think, forcible, as compared with most religious writing; especially in its frankness and fearlessness: but it was wholly mistaken: for I had been educated in the doctrines of a narrow sect, and had read history as obliquely as sectarians necessarily must.

Mingled among these either unnecessary or erroneous statements, I find, indeed, some that might be still of value; but these, in my earlier books, disfigured by affected language, partly through the desire to be thought a fine writer, and partly, as in the second volume of 'Modern Painters, ' in the notion of returning as far as I could to what I thought the better style of old English literature, especially to that of my then favourite, in prose, Richard Hooker.

For these reasons, —though, as respects either art, policy, or morality, as distinct from religion, I not only still hold, but would even wish strongly to re-affirm the substance of what I said in my earliest books, —I shall reprint scarcely anything in this series out of the first and second volumes of 'Modern Painters'; and shall omit much of the 'Seven Lamps' and 'Stones of Venice'; but all my books written within the last fifteen years will be republished without change, as new editions of them are called for, with here and there perhaps an additional note, and having their text divided, for convenient reference, into paragraphs, consecutive through each volume. I shall also throw together the shorter fragments that bear on each other, and fill in with such unprinted lectures or studies as seem to me worth preserving, so as to keep the volumes, on an average, composed of about a hundred leaves each.

The first book of which a new edition is required chances to be 'Sesame and Lilies, ' from which I now detach the whole preface, about the Alps, for use elsewhere; and to I which I add a lecture given in Ireland on a subject closely connected with that of the book itself. I am glad that it should be the first of the complete series, for many reasons; though in now looking over these two lectures, I am painfully struck by the waste of good work in them. They cost me much thought, and much strong emotion; but it was foolish to suppose that I could rouse my audiences in a little while to any sympathy with the temper into which I had brought myself by years of thinking over subjects full of pain; while, if I missed my purpose at the time, it was little to be hoped I could attain it afterwards; since phrases written for oral delivery become ineffective when quietly read. Yet I should only take away what good is in them if I tried to translate them into the language of books; nor, indeed, could I at all have done so at the time of their delivery, my thoughts then habitually and impatiently putting themselves into forms fit only for emphatic speech; and thus I am startled, in my review of them, to find that, though there is much, (forgive me the impertinence) which seems to me accurately and energetically said, there is scarcely anything put in a form to be generally convincing, or even easily intelligible: and I can well imagine a reader laying down the book without being at all moved by it, still less guided, to any definite course of action.

I think, however, if I now say briefly and clearly what I meant my hearers to understand, and what I wanted, and still would fain have, them to do, there may afterwards be found some better service in the passionately written text.

The first lecture says, or tries to say, that, life being very short, and the quiet hours of it few, we ought to waste none of them in reading valueless books; and that valuable books should, in a civilized country, be within the reach of every one, printed in excellent form, for a just price; but not in any vile, vulgar, or, by reason of smallness of type, physically injurious form, at a vile price. For we none of us need many books, and those which we need ought to be clearly printed, on the best paper, and strongly bound. And though we are, indeed, now, a wretched and poverty-struck nation, and hardly able to keep soul and body together, still, as no person in decent circumstances would put on his table confessedly bad wine, or bad meat, without being ashamed, so he need not have on his shelves ill-printed or loosely and wretchedly-stitched books; for though few can be rich, yet every man who honestly exerts himself may, I think, still provide, for himself and his family, good shoes, good gloves, strong harness for his cart or carriage horses, and stout leather binding for his books. And I would urge upon every young man, as the beginning of his due and wise provision for his household, to obtain as soon as he can, by the severest economy, a restricted, serviceable, and steadily—however slowly— increasing, series of books for use through life; making his little library, of all the furniture in his room, the most studied and decorative piece; every volume having its assigned place, like a little statue in its niche, and one of the earliest and strictest lessons to the children of the house being how to turn the pages of their own literary possessions lightly and deliberately, with no chance of tearing or dog's ears.

That is my notion of the founding of Kings' Treasuries; and the first lecture is intended to show somewhat the use and preciousness of their treasures: but the two following ones have wider scope, being written in the hope of awakening the youth of England, so far as my poor words might have any power with them, to take some thought of the purposes of the life into which they are entering, and the nature of the world they have to conquer.

These two lectures are fragmentary and ill-arranged, but not, I think, diffuse or much compressible. The entire gist and conclusion of them, however, is in the last six paragraphs of the third lecture, which I would beg the reader to look over not once nor twice, (rather than any other part of the book,) for they contain the best expression I have yet been able to put in words of what, so far as is within my power, I mean henceforward both to do myself, and to plead with all over whom I have any influence, to do also according to their means: the letters begun on the first day of this year, to the workmen of England, having the object of originating, if possible, this movement among them, in true alliance with whatever trustworthy element of help they can find in the higher classes. After these paragraphs, let me ask you to read, by the fiery light of recent events, the fable at p. 170 {1}, and then paragraphs 129-131 {2}; and observe, my statement respecting the famine at Orissa is not rhetorical, but certified by official documents as within the truth. Five hundred thousand persons, AT LEAST, died by starvation in our British dominions, wholly in consequence of carelessness and want of forethought. Keep that well in your memory; and note it as the best possible illustration of modern political economy in true practice, and of the relations it has accomplished between Supply and Demand. Then begin the second lecture, and all will read clear enough, I think, to the end; only, since that second lecture was written, questions have arisen respecting the education and claims of women which have greatly troubled simple minds and excited restless ones. I am sometimes asked my thoughts on this matter, and I suppose that some girl readers of the second lecture may at the end of it desire to be told summarily what I would have them do and desire in the present state of things. This, then, is what I would say to any girl who had confidence enough in me to believe what I told her, or to do what I asked her.

First, be quite sure of one thing, that, however much you may know, and whatever advantages you may possess, and however good you may be, you have not been singled out, by the God who made you, from all the other girls in the world, to be especially informed respecting His own nature and character. You have not been born in a luminous point upon the surface of the globe, where a perfect theology might be expounded to you from your youth up, and where everything you were taught would be true, and everything that was enforced upon you, right. Of all the insolent, all the foolish persuasions that by any chance could enter and hold your empty little heart, this is the proudest and foolishest, —that you have been so much the darling of the Heavens, and favourite of the Fates, as to be born in the very nick of time, and in the punctual place, when and where pure Divine truth had been sifted from the errors of the Nations; and that your papa had been providentially disposed to buy a house in the convenient neighbourhood of the steeple under which that Immaculate and final verity would be beautifully proclaimed. Do not think it, child; it is not so. This, on the contrary, is the fact, - -unpleasant you may think it; pleasant, it seems to ME, —that you, with all your pretty dresses, and dainty looks, and kindly thoughts, and saintly aspirations, are not one whit more thought of or loved by the great Maker and Master than any poor little red, black, or blue savage, running wild in the pestilent woods, or naked on the hot sands of the earth: and that, of the two, you probably know less about God than she does; the only difference being that she thinks little of Him that is right, and you much that is wrong.

That, then, is the first thing to make sure of; —that you are not yet perfectly well informed on the most abstruse of all possible subjects, and that if you care to behave with modesty or propriety, you had better be silent about it.

The second thing which you may make sure of is, that however good you may be, you have faults; that however dull you may be, you can find out what some of them are; and that however slight they may be, you had better make some—not too painful, but patient—effort to get quit of them. And so far as you have confidence in me at all, trust me for this, that how many soever you may find or fancy your faults to be, there are only two that are of real consequence, — Idleness and Cruelty. Perhaps you may be proud. Well, we can get much good out of pride, if only it be not religious. Perhaps you may be vain; it is highly probable; and very pleasant for the people who like to praise you. Perhaps you are a little envious: that is really very shocking; but then—so is everybody else. Perhaps, also, you are a little malicious, which I am truly concerned to hear, but should probably only the more, if I knew you, enjoy your conversation. But whatever else you may be, you must not be useless, and you must not be cruel. If there is any one point which, in six thousand years of thinking about right and wrong, wise and good men have agreed upon, or successively by experience discovered, it is that God dislikes idle and cruel people more than any others: - that His first order is, "Work while you have light; " and His second, "Be merciful while you have mercy. "

"Work while you have light, " especially while you have the light of morning. There are few things more wonderful to me than that old people never tell young ones how precious their youth is. They sometimes sentimentally regret their own earlier days; sometimes prudently forget them; often foolishly rebuke the young, often more foolishly indulge, often most foolishly thwart and restrain; but scarcely ever warn or watch them. Remember, then, that I, at least, have warned YOU, that the happiness of your life, and its power, and its part and rank in earth or in heaven, depend on the way you pass your days now. They are not to be sad days: far from that, the first duty of young people is to be delighted and delightful; but they are to be in the deepest sense solemn days. There is no solemnity so deep, to a rightly-thinking creature, as that of dawn. But not only in that beautiful sense, but in all their character and method, they are to be solemn days. Take your Latin dictionary, and look out "solennis, " and fix the sense of the word well in your mind, and remember that every day of your early life is ordaining irrevocably, for good or evil, the custom and practice of your soul; ordaining either sacred customs of dear and lovely recurrence, or trenching deeper and deeper the furrows for seed of sorrow. Now, therefore, see that no day passes in which you do not make yourself a somewhat better creature: and in order to do that, find out, first, what you are now. Do not think vaguely about it; take pen and paper, and write down as accurate a description of yourself as you can, with the date to it. If you dare not do so, find out why you dare not, and try to get strength of heart enough to look yourself fairly in the face in mind as well as body. I do not doubt but that the mind is a less pleasant thing to look at than the face, and for that very reason it needs more looking at; so always have two mirrors on your toilet table, and see that with proper care you dress body and mind before them daily. After the dressing is once over for the day, think no more about it: as your hair will blow about your ears, so your temper and thoughts will get ruffled with the day's work, and may need, sometimes, twice dressing; but I don't want you to carry about a mental pocket-comb; only to be smooth braided always in the morning.

Write down then, frankly, what you are, or, at least, what you think yourself, not dwelling upon those inevitable faults which I have just told you are of little consequence, and which the action of a right life will shake or smooth away; but that you may determine to the best of your intelligence what you are good for and can be made into. You will find that the mere resolve not to be useless, and the honest desire to help other people, will, in the quickest and delicatest ways, improve yourself. Thus, from the beginning, consider all your accomplishments as means of assistance to others; read attentively, in this volume, paragraphs 74, 75, 19, and 79, {3} and you will understand what I mean, with respect to languages and music. In music especially you will soon find what personal benefit there is in being serviceable: it is probable that, however limited your powers, you have voice and ear enough to sustain a note of moderate compass in a concerted piece; —that, then, is the first thing to make sure you can do. Get your voice disciplined and clear, and think only of accuracy; never of effect or expression: if you have any soul worth expressing, it will show itself in your singing; but most likely there are very few feelings in you, at present, needing any particular expression; and the one thing you have to do is to make a clear-voiced little instrument of yourself, which other people can entirely depend upon for the note wanted. So, in drawing, as soon as you can set down the right shape of anything, and thereby explain its character to another person, or make the look of it clear and interesting to a child, you will begin to enjoy the art vividly for its own sake, and all your habits of mind and powers of memory will gain precision: but if you only try to make showy drawings for praise, or pretty ones for amusement, your drawing will have little of real interest for you, and no educational power whatever.

Then, besides this more delicate work, resolve to do every day some that is useful in the vulgar sense. Learn first thoroughly the economy of the kitchen; the good and bad qualities of every common article of food, and the simplest and best modes of their preparation: when you have time, go and help in the cooking of poorer families, and show them how to make as much of everything as possible, and how to make little, nice; coaxing and tempting them into tidy and pretty ways, and pleading for well-folded table- cloths, however coarse, and for a flower or two out of the garden to strew on them. If you manage to get a clean table-cloth, bright plates on it, and a good dish in the middle, of your own cooking, you may ask leave to say a short grace; and let your religious ministries be confined to that much for the present.

Again, let a certain part of your day (as little as you choose, but not to be broken in upon) be set apart for making strong and pretty dresses for the poor. Learn the sound qualities of all useful stuffs, and make everything of the best you can get, whatever its price. I have many reasons for desiring you to do this, —too many to be told just now, —trust me, and be sure you get everything as good as can be: and if, in the villainous state of modern trade, you cannot get it good at any price, buy its raw material, and set some of the poor women about you to spin and weave, till you have got stuff that can be trusted: and then, every day, make some little piece of useful clothing, sewn with your own fingers as strongly as it can be stitched; and embroider it or otherwise beautify it moderately with fine needlework, such as a girl may be proud of having done. And accumulate these things by you until you hear of some honest persons in need of clothing, which may often too sorrowfully be; and, even though you should be deceived, and give them to the dishonest, and hear of their being at once taken to the pawnbroker's, never mind that, for the pawnbroker must sell them to some one who has need of them. That is no business of yours; what concerns you is only that when you see a half-naked child, you should have good and fresh clothes to give it, if its parents will let it be taught to wear them. If they will not, consider how they came to be of such a mind, which it will be wholesome for you beyond most subjects of inquiry to ascertain. And after you have gone on doing this a little while, you will begin to understand the meaning of at least one chapter of your Bible, Proverbs xxxi., without need of any laboured comment, sermon, or meditation.

In these, then (and of course in all minor ways besides, that you can discover in your own household), you must be to the best of your strength usefully employed during the greater part of the day, so that you may be able at the end of it to say, as proudly as any peasant, that you have not eaten the bread of idleness.

Then, secondly, I said, you are not to be cruel. Perhaps you think there is no chance of your being so; and indeed I hope it is not likely that you should be deliberately unkind to any creature; but unless you are deliberately kind to every creature, you will often be cruel to many. Cruel, partly through want of imagination, (a far rarer and weaker faculty in women than men,) and yet more, at the present day, through the subtle encouragement of your selfishness by the religious doctrine that all which we now suppose to be evil will be brought to a good end; doctrine practically issuing, not in less earnest efforts that the immediate unpleasantness may be averted from ourselves, but in our remaining satisfied in the contemplation of its ultimate objects, when it is inflicted on others.

It is not likely that the more accurate methods of recent mental education will now long permit young people to grow up in the persuasion that, in any danger or distress, they may expect to be themselves saved by the Providence of God, while those around them are lost by His improvidence: but they may be yet long restrained from rightly kind action, and long accustomed to endure both their own pain occasionally, and the pain of others always, with an unwise patience, by misconception of the eternal and incurable nature of real evil. Observe, therefore, carefully in this matter; there are degrees of pain, as degrees of faultfulness, which are altogether conquerable, and which seem to be merely forms of wholesome trial or discipline. Your fingers tingle when you go out on a frosty morning, and are all the warmer afterwards; your limbs are weary with wholesome work, and lie down in the pleasanter rest; you are tried for a little while by having to wait for some promised good, and it is all the sweeter when it comes. But you cannot carry the trial past a certain point. Let the cold fasten on your hand in an extreme degree, and your fingers will moulder from their sockets. Fatigue yourself, but once, to utter exhaustion, and to the end of life you shall not recover the former vigour of your frame. Let heart-sickness pass beyond a certain bitter point, and the heart loses its life for ever.

Now, the very definition of evil is in this irremediableness. It means sorrow, or sin, which ends in death; and assuredly, as far as we know, or can conceive, there are many conditions both of pain and sin which cannot but so end. Of course we are ignorant and blind creatures, and we cannot know what seeds of good may be in present suffering, or present crime; but with what we cannot know we are not concerned. It is conceivable that murderers and liars may in some distant world be exalted into a higher humanity than they could have reached without homicide or falsehood; but the contingency is not one by which our actions should be guided. There is, indeed, a better hope that the beggar, who lies at our gates in misery, may, within gates of pearl, be comforted; but the Master, whose words are our only authority for thinking so, never Himself inflicted disease as a blessing, nor sent away the hungry unfed, or the wounded unhealed.

Believe me then, the only right principle of action here, is to consider good and evil as defined by our natural sense of both; and to strive to promote the one, and to conquer the other, with as hearty endeavour as if there were, indeed, no other world than this. Above all, get quit of the absurd idea that Heaven will interfere to correct great errors, while allowing its laws to take their course in punishing small ones. If you prepare a dish of food carelessly, you do not expect Providence to make it palatable; neither if, through years of folly, you misguide your own life, need you expect Divine interference to bring round everything at last for the best. I tell you, positively, the world is not so constituted: the consequences of great mistakes are just as sure as those of small ones, and the happiness of your whole life, and of all the lives over which you have power, depend as literally on your own common sense and discretion as the excellence and order of the feast of a day.

Think carefully and bravely over these things, and you will find them true: having found them so, think also carefully over your own position in life. I assume that you belong to the middle or upper classes, and that you would shrink from descending into a lower sphere. You may fancy you would not: nay, if you are very good, strong-hearted, and romantic, perhaps you really would not; but it is not wrong that you should. You have, then, I suppose, good food, pretty rooms to live in, pretty dresses to wear, power of obtaining every rational and wholesome pleasure; you are, moreover, probably gentle and grateful, and in the habit of every day thanking God for these things. But why do you thank Him? Is it because, in these matters, as well as in your religious knowledge, you think He has made a favourite of you? Is the essential meaning of your thanksgiving, "Lord, I thank Thee that I am not as other girls are, not in that I fast twice in the week while they feast, but in that I feast seven times a week while they fast, " and are you quite sure this is a pleasing form of thanksgiving to your Heavenly Father? Suppose you saw one of your own true earthly sisters, Lucy or Emily, cast out of your mortal father's house, starving, helpless, heartbroken; and that every morning when you went into your father's room, you said to him, "How good you are, father, to give me what you don't give Lucy, " are you sure that, whatever anger your parent might have just cause for, against your sister, he would be pleased by that thanksgiving, or flattered by that praise? Nay, are you even sure that you ARE so much the favourite? —suppose that, all this while, he loves poor Lucy just as well as you, and is only trying you through her pain, and perhaps not angry with her in anywise, but deeply angry with you, and all the more for your thanksgivings? Would it not be well that you should think, and earnestly too, over this standing of yours; and all the more if you wish to believe that text, which clergymen so much dislike preaching on, "How hardly shall they that have riches enter into the Kingdom of God"? You do not believe it now, or you would be less complacent in your state; and you cannot believe it at all, until you know that the Kingdom of God means, —"not meat and drink, but justice, peace, and joy in the Holy Ghost, " nor until you know also that such joy is not by any means, necessarily, in going to church, or in singing hymns; but may be joy in a dance, or joy in a jest, or joy in anything you have deserved to possess, or that you are willing to give; but joy in nothing that separates you, as by any strange favour, from your fellow-creatures, that exalts you through their degradation—exempts you from their toil—or indulges you in time of their distress.

Think, then, and some day, I believe, you will feel also, —no morbid passion of pity such as would turn you into a black Sister of Charity, but the steady fire of perpetual kindness which will make you a bright one. I speak in no disparagement of them; I know well how good the Sisters of Charity are, and how much we owe to them; but all these professional pieties (except so far as distinction or association may be necessary for effectiveness of work) are in their spirit wrong, and in practice merely plaster the sores of disease that ought never to have been permitted to exist; encouraging at the same time the herd of less excellent women in frivolity, by leading them to think that they must either be good up to the black standard, or cannot be good for anything. Wear a costume, by all means, if you like; but let it be a cheerful and becoming one; and be in your heart a Sister of Charity always, without either veiled or voluble declaration of it.

As I pause, before ending my preface—thinking of one or two more points that are difficult to write of—I find a letter in 'The Times, ' from a French lady, which says all I want so beautifully, that I will print it just as it stands: -

SIR, —It is often said that one example is worth many sermons. Shall I be judged presumptuous if I point out one, which seems to me so striking just now, that, however painful, I cannot help dwelling upon it?

It is the share, the sad and large share, that French society and its recent habits of luxury, of expenses, of dress, of indulgence in every kind of extravagant dissipation, has to lay to its own door in its actual crisis of ruin, misery, and humiliation. If our MENAGERES can be cited as an example to English housewives, so, alas! can other classes of our society be set up as an example—NOT to be followed.

Bitter must be the feelings of many a French woman whose days of luxury and expensive habits are at an end, and whose bills of bygone splendour lie with a heavy weight on her conscience, if not on her purse!

With us the evil has spread high and low. Everywhere have the examples given by the highest ladies in the land been followed but too successfully.

Every year did dress become more extravagant, entertainments more costly, expenses of every kind more considerable. Lower and lower became the tone of society, its good breeding, its delicacy. More and more were MONDE and DEMI-MONDE associated in newspaper accounts of fashionable doings, in scandalous gossip, on racecourses, in PREMIERES REPRESENTATIONS, in imitation of each other's costumes, MOBILIERS and slang.

Living beyond one's means became habitual—almost necessary—for every one to keep up with, if not to go beyond, every one else.

What the result of all this has been we now see in the wreck of our prosperity, in the downfall of all that seemed brightest and highest.

Deeply and fearfully impressed by what my own country has incurred and is suffering, I cannot help feeling sorrowful when I see in England signs of our besetting sins appearing also. Paint and chignons, slang and vaudevilles, knowing "Anonymas" by name, and reading doubtfully moral novels, are in themselves small offences, although not many years ago they would have appeared very heinous ones, yet they are quick and tempting conveyances on a very dangerous high-road.

I would that all Englishwomen knew how they are looked up to from abroad—what a high opinion, what honour and reverence we foreigners have for their principles, their truthfulness, the fresh and pure innocence of their daughters, the healthy youthfulness of their lovely children.

May I illustrate this by a short example which happened very near me? During the days of the EMEUTES of 1848, all the houses in Paris were being searched for firearms by the mob. The one I was living in contained none, as the master of the house repeatedly assured the furious and incredulous Republicans. They were going to lay violent hands on him when his wife, an English lady, hearing the loud discussion, came bravely forward and assured them that no arms were concealed. "Vous etes anglaise, nous vous croyons; les anglaises disent toujours la verite, " was the immediate answer, and the rioters quietly left.

Now, Sir, shall I be accused of unjustified criticism if, loving and admiring your country, as these lines will prove, certain new features strike me as painful discrepancies in English life?

Far be it from me to preach the contempt of all that can make life lovable and wholesomely pleasant. I love nothing better than to see a woman nice, neat, elegant, looking her best in the prettiest dress that her taste and purse can afford, or your bright, fresh young girls fearlessly and perfectly sitting their horses, or adorning their houses as pretty [sic; it is not quite grammar, but it is better than if it were;] as care, trouble, and refinement can make them.

It is the degree BEYOND that which to us has proved so fatal, and that I would our example could warn you from as a small repayment for your hospitality and friendliness to us in our days of trouble.

May Englishwomen accept this in a kindly spirit as a New-year's wish from

A FRENCH LADY. Dec. 29.

That, then, is the substance of what I would fain say convincingly, if it might be, to my girl friends; at all events with certainty in my own mind that I was thus far a safe guide to them.

For other and older readers it is needful I should write a few words more, respecting what opportunity I have had to judge, or right I have to speak, of such things; for, indeed, too much of what I have said about women has been said in faith only. A wise and lovely English lady told me, when 'Sesame and Lilies' first appeared, that she was sure the 'Sesame' would be useful, but that in the 'Lilies' I had been writing of what I knew nothing about. Which was in a measure too true, and also that it is more partial than my writings are usually: for as Ellesmere spoke his speech on the— intervention, not, indeed, otherwise than he felt, but yet altogether for the sake of Gretchen, so I wrote the 'Lilies' to please one girl; and were it not for what I remember of her, and of few besides, should now perhaps recast some of the sentences in the 'Lilies' in a very different tone: for as years have gone by, it has chanced to me, untowardly in some respects, fortunately in others (because it enables me to read history more clearly), to see the utmost evil that is in women, while I have had but to believe the utmost good. The best women are indeed necessarily the most difficult to know; they are recognized chiefly in the happiness of their husbands and the nobleness of their children; they are only to be divined, not discerned, by the stranger; and, sometimes, seem almost helpless except in their homes; yet without the help of one of them, {4} to whom this book is dedicated, the day would probably have come before now, when I should have written and thought no more.

On the other hand, the fashion of the time renders whatever is forward, coarse, or senseless, in feminine nature, too palpable to all men: - the weak picturesqueness of my earlier writings brought me acquainted with much of their emptiest enthusiasm; and the chances of later life gave me opportunities of watching women in states of degradation and vindictiveness which opened to me the gloomiest secrets of Greek and Syrian tragedy. I have seen them betray their household charities to lust, their pledged love to devotion; I have seen mothers dutiful to their children, as Medea; and children dutiful to their parents, as the daughter of Herodias: but my trust is still unmoved in the preciousness of the natures that are so fatal in their error, and I leave the words of the 'Lilies' unchanged; believing, yet, that no man ever lived a right life who had not been chastened by a woman's love, strengthened by her courage, and guided by her discretion.

What I might myself have been, so helped, I rarely indulge in the idleness of thinking; but what I am, since I take on me the function of a teacher, it is well that the reader should know, as far as I can tell him.

Not an unjust person; not an unkind one; not a false one; a lover of order, labour, and peace. That, it seems to me, is enough to give me right to say all I care to say on ethical subjects; more, I could only tell definitely through details of autobiography such as none but prosperous and (in the simple sense of the word) faultless lives could justify; —and mine has been neither. Yet, if any one, skilled in reading the torn manuscripts of the human soul, cares for more intimate knowledge of me, he may have it by knowing with what persons in past history I have most sympathy.

I will name three.

In all that is strongest and deepest in me, —that fits me for my work, and gives light or shadow to my being, I have sympathy with Guido Guinicelli.

In my constant natural temper, and thoughts of things and of people, with Marmontel.

In my enforced and accidental temper, and thoughts of things and of people, with Dean Swift.

Any one who can understand the natures of those three men, can understand mine; and having said so much, I am content to leave both life and work to be remembered or forgotten, as their uses may deserve.

DENMARK HILL,

1st January, 1871.

LECTURE III—THE MYSTERY OF LIFE AND ITS ARTS

Lecture delivered in the theatre of the Royal College of Science, Dublin, 1868.

When I accepted the privilege of addressing you to-day, I was not aware of a restriction with respect to the topics of discussion which may be brought before this Society {29}—a restriction which, though entirely wise and right under the circumstances contemplated in its introduction, would necessarily have disabled me, thinking as I think, from preparing any lecture for you on the subject of art in a form which might be permanently useful. Pardon me, therefore, in so far as I must transgress such limitation; for indeed my infringement will be of the letter—not of the spirit—of your commands. In whatever I may say touching the religion which has been the foundation of art, or the policy which has contributed to its power, if I offend one, I shall offend all; for I shall take no note of any separations in creeds, or antagonisms in parties: neither do I fear that ultimately I shall offend any, by proving—or at least stating as capable of positive proof—the connection of all that is best in the crafts and arts of man, with the simplicity of his faith, and the sincerity of his patriotism.

But I speak to you under another disadvantage, by which I am checked in frankness of utterance, not here only, but everywhere: namely, that I am never fully aware how far my audiences are disposed to give me credit for real knowledge of my subject, or how far they grant me attention only because I have been sometimes thought an ingenious or pleasant essayist upon it. For I have had what, in many respects, I boldly call the misfortune, to set my words sometimes prettily together; not without a foolish vanity in the poor knack that I had of doing so: until I was heavily punished for this pride, by finding that many people thought of the words only, and cared nothing for their meaning. Happily, therefore, the power of using such pleasant language—if indeed it ever were mine—is passing away from me; and whatever I am now able to say at all, I find myself forced to say with great plainness. For my thoughts have changed also, as my words have; and whereas in earlier life, what little influence I obtained was due perhaps chiefly to the enthusiasm with which I was able to dwell on the beauty of the physical clouds, and of their colours in the sky; so all the influence I now desire to retain must be due to the earnestness with which I am endeavouring to trace the form and beauty of another kind of cloud than those; the bright cloud of which it is written—"What is your life? It is even as a vapour that appeareth for a little time, and then vanisheth away. "

I suppose few people reach the middle or latter period of their age, without having, at some moment of change or disappointment, felt the truth of those bitter words; and been startled by the fading of the sunshine from the cloud of their life into the sudden agony of the knowledge that the fabric of it was as fragile as a dream, and the endurance of it as transient as the dew. But it is not always that, even at such times of melancholy surprise, we can enter into any true perception that this human life shares in the nature of it, not only the evanescence, but the mystery of the cloud; that its avenues are wreathed in darkness, and its forms and courses no less fantastic, than spectral and obscure; so that not only in the vanity which we cannot grasp, but in the shadow which we cannot pierce, it is true of this cloudy life of ours, that "man walketh in a vain shadow, and disquieteth himself in vain. "

And least of all, whatever may have been the eagerness of our passions, or the height of our pride, are we able to understand in its depth the third and most solemn character in which our life is like those clouds of heaven; that to it belongs not only their transcience, not only their mystery, but also their power; that in the cloud of the human soul there is a fire stronger than the lightning, and a grace more precious than the rain; and that though of the good and evil it shall one day be said alike, that the place that knew them knows them no more, there is an infinite separation between those whose brief presence had there been a blessing, like the mist of Eden that went up from the earth to water the garden, and those whose place knew them only as a drifting and changeful shade, of whom the heavenly sentence is, that they are "wells without water; clouds that are carried with a tempest, to whom the mist of darkness is reserved for ever. "

To those among us, however, who have lived long enough to form some just estimate of the rate of the changes which are, hour by hour in accelerating catastrophe, manifesting themselves in the laws, the arts, and the creeds of men, it seems to me, that now at least, if never at any former time, the thoughts of the true nature of our life, and of its powers and responsibilities, should present themselves with absolute sadness and sternness. And although I know that this feeling is much deepened in my own mind by disappointment, which, by chance, has attended the greater number of my cherished purposes, I do not for that reason distrust the feeling itself, though I am on my guard against an exaggerated degree of it: nay, I rather believe that in periods of new effort and violent change, disappointment is a wholesome medicine; and that in the secret of it, as in the twilight so beloved by Titian, we may see the colours of things with deeper truth than in the most dazzling sunshine. And because these truths about the works of men, which I want to bring to-day before you, are most of them sad ones, though at the same time helpful; and because also I believe that your kind Irish hearts will answer more gladly to the truthful expression of a personal feeling, than to the exposition of an abstract principle, I will permit myself so much unreserved speaking of my own causes of regret, as may enable you to make just allowance for what, according to your sympathies, you will call either the bitterness, or the insight, of a mind which has surrendered its best hopes, and been foiled in its favourite aims.

I spent the ten strongest years of my life, (from twenty to thirty,) in endeavouring to show the excellence of the work of the man whom I believed, and rightly believed, to be the greatest painter of the schools of England since Reynolds. I had then perfect faith in the power of every great truth of beauty to prevail ultimately, and take its right place in usefulness and honour; and I strove to bring the painter's work into this due place, while the painter was yet alive. But he knew, better than I, the uselessness of talking about what people could not see for themselves. He always discouraged me scornfully, even when he thanked me—and he died before even the superficial effect of my work was visible. I went on, however, thinking I could at least be of use to the public, if not to him, in proving his power. My books got talked about a little. The prices of modern pictures, generally, rose, and I was beginning to take some pleasure in a sense of gradual victory, when, fortunately or unfortunately, an opportunity of perfect trial undeceived me at once, and for ever. The Trustees of the National Gallery commissioned me to arrange the Turner drawings there, and permitted me to prepare three hundred examples of his studies from nature, for exhibition at Kensington. At Kensington they were, and are, placed for exhibition; but they are not exhibited, for the room in which they hang is always empty.

Well—this showed me at once, that those ten years of my life had been, in their chief purpose, lost. For that, I did not so much care; I had, at least, learned my own business thoroughly, and should be able, as I fondly supposed, after such a lesson, now to use my knowledge with better effect. But what I did care for was the—to me frightful—discovery, that the most splendid genius in the arts might be permitted by Providence to labour and perish uselessly; that in the very fineness of it there might be something rendering it invisible to ordinary eyes; but that, with this strange excellence, faults might be mingled which would be as deadly as its virtues were vain; that the glory of it was perishable, as well as invisible, and the gift and grace of it might be to us as snow in summer and as rain in harvest.

That was the first mystery of life to me. But, while my best energy was given to the study of painting, I had put collateral effort, more prudent if less enthusiastic, into that of architecture; and in this I could not complain of meeting with no sympathy. Among several personal reasons which caused me to desire that I might give this, my closing lecture on the subject of art here, in Ireland, one of the chief was, that in reading it, I should stand near the beautiful building, —the engineer's school of your college, —which was the first realization I had the joy to see, of the principles I had, until then, been endeavouring to teach! but which, alas, is now, to me, no more than the richly canopied monument of one of the most earnest souls that ever gave itself to the arts, and one of my truest and most loving friends, Benjamin Woodward. Nor was it here in Ireland only that I received the help of Irish sympathy and genius. When to another friend, Sir Thomas Deane, with Mr. Woodward, was entrusted the building of the museum at Oxford, the best details of the work were executed by sculptors who had been born and trained here; and the first window of the facade of the building, in which was inaugurated the study of natural science in England, in true fellowship with literature, was carved from my design by an Irish sculptor.

You may perhaps think that no man ought to speak of disappointment, to whom, even in one branch of labour, so much success was granted. Had Mr. Woodward now been beside me, I had not so spoken; but his gentle and passionate spirit was cut off from the fulfilment of its purposes, and the work we did together is now become vain. It may not be so in future; but the architecture we endeavoured to introduce is inconsistent alike with the reckless luxury, the deforming mechanism, and the squalid misery of modern cities; among the formative fashions of the day, aided, especially in England, by ecclesiastical sentiment, it indeed obtained notoriety; and sometimes behind an engine furnace, or a railroad bank, you may detect the pathetic discord of its momentary grace, and, with toil, decipher its floral carvings choked with soot. I felt answerable to the schools I loved, only for their injury. I perceived that this new portion of my strength had also been spent in vain; and from amidst streets of iron, and palaces of crystal, shrank back at last to the carving of the mountain and colour of the flower.

And still I could tell of failure, and failure repeated, as years went on; but I have trespassed enough on your patience to show you, in part, the causes of my discouragement. Now let me more deliberately tell you its results. You know there is a tendency in the minds of many men, when they are heavily disappointed in the main purposes of their life, to feel, and perhaps in warning, perhaps in mockery, to declare, that life itself is a vanity. Because it has disappointed them, they think its nature is of disappointment always, or at best, of pleasure that can be grasped by imagination only; that the cloud of it has no strength nor fire within; but is a painted cloud only, to be delighted in, yet despised. You know how beautifully Pope has expressed this particular phase of thought: -

> "Meanwhile opinion gilds, with varying rays,
> These painted clouds that beautify our days;
> Each want of happiness by hope supplied,
> And each vacuity of sense, by pride.
> Hope builds as fast as Knowledge can destroy;
> In Folly's cup, still laughs the bubble joy.
> One pleasure past, another still we gain,
> And not a vanity is given in vain."

But the effect of failure upon my own mind has been just the reverse of this. The more that my life disappointed me, the more solemn and wonderful it became to me. It seemed, contrarily to Pope's saying, that the vanity of it WAS indeed given in vain; but that there was something behind the veil of it, which was not vanity. It became to me not a painted cloud, but a terrible and impenetrable one: not a mirage, which vanished as I drew near, but a pillar of darkness, to which I was forbidden to draw near. For I saw that both my own failure, and such success in petty things as in its poor triumph seemed to me worse than failure, came from the want of sufficiently earnest effort to understand the whole law and meaning of existence, and to bring it to noble and due end; as, on the other hand, I saw more and more clearly that all enduring success in the arts, or in any other occupation, had come from the ruling of lower purposes, not by a conviction of their nothingness, but by a solemn faith in the advancing power of human nature, or in the promise, however dimly apprehended, that the mortal part of it would one day be swallowed up in immortality; and that, indeed, the arts themselves never had reached any vital strength or honour, but in the effort to proclaim this immortality, and in the service either of great and just religion, or of some unselfish patriotism, and law of such national life as must be the foundation of religion.

Nothing that I have ever said is more true or necessary—nothing has been more misunderstood or misapplied—than my strong assertion that the arts can never be right themselves, unless their motive is right. It is misunderstood this way: weak painters, who have never learned their business, and cannot lay a true line, continually come to me, crying out—"Look at this picture of mine; it MUST be good, I had such a lovely motive. I have put my whole heart into it, and taken years to think over its treatment. " Well, the only answer for these people is—if one had the cruelty to make it—"Sir, you cannot think over ANYthing in any number of years, —you haven't the head to do it; and though you had fine motives, strong enough to make you burn yourself in a slow fire, if only first you could paint a picture, you can't paint one, nor half an inch of one; you haven't the hand to do it. "

But, far more decisively we have to say to the men who DO know their business, or may know it if they choose—"Sir, you have this gift, and a mighty one; see that you serve your nation faithfully with it. It is a greater trust than ships and armies: you might cast THEM away, if you were their captain, with less treason to your people than in casting your own glorious power away, and serving the devil with it instead of men. Ships and armies you may replace if they are lost, but a great intellect, once abused, is a curse to the earth for ever. "

This, then, I meant by saying that the arts must have noble motive. This also I said respecting them, that they never had prospered, nor could prosper, but when they had such true purpose, and were devoted to the proclamation of divine truth or law. And yet I saw also that they had always failed in this proclamation—that poetry, and sculpture, and painting, though only great when they strove to teach us something about the gods, never had taught us anything trustworthy about the gods, but had always betrayed their trust in the crisis of it, and, with their powers at the full reach, became ministers to pride and to lust. And I felt also, with increasing amazement, the unconquerable apathy in ourselves and hearers, no less than in these the teachers; and that while the wisdom and rightness of every act and art of life could only be consistent with a right understanding of the ends of life, we were all plunged as in a languid dream—our hearts fat, and our eyes heavy, and our ears closed, lest the inspiration of hand or voice should reach us—lest we should see with our eyes, and understand with our hearts, and be healed.

This intense apathy in all of us is the first great mystery of life; it stands in the way of every perception, every virtue. There is no making ourselves feel enough astonishment at it. That the occupations or pastimes of life should have no motive, is understandable; but—That life itself should have no motive—that we neither care to find out what it may lead to, nor to guard against its being for ever taken away from us—here is a mystery indeed. For just suppose I were able to call at this moment to any one in this audience by name, and to tell him positively that I knew a large estate had been lately left to him on some curious conditions; but that though I knew it was large, I did not know how large, nor even where it was—whether in the East Indies or the West, or in England, or at the Antipodes. I only knew it was a vast estate, and that there was a chance of his losing it altogether if he did not soon find out on what terms it had been left to him. Suppose I were able to say this positively to any single man in this audience, and he knew that I did not speak without warrant, do you think that he would rest content with that vague knowledge, if it were anywise possible to obtain more? Would he not give every energy to find some trace of the facts, and never rest till he had ascertained where this place was, and what it was like? And suppose he were a young man, and all he could discover by his best endeavour was that the estate was never to be his at all, unless he persevered, during certain years of probation, in an orderly and industrious life; but that, according to the rightness of his conduct, the portion of the estate assigned to him would be greater or less, so that it literally depended on his behaviour from day to day whether he got ten thousand a year, or thirty thousand a year, or nothing whatever- -would you not think it strange if the youth never troubled himself to satisfy the conditions in any way, nor even to know what was required of him, but lived exactly as he chose, and never inquired whether his chances of the estate were increasing or passing away? Well, you know that this is actually and literally so with the greater number of the educated persons now living in Christian countries. Nearly every man and woman in any company such as this, outwardly professes to believe—and a large number unquestionably think they believe—much more than this; not only that a quite unlimited estate is in prospect for them if they please the Holder of it, but that the infinite contrary of such a possession—an estate of perpetual misery—is in store for them if they displease this great Land-Holder, this great Heaven-Holder. And yet there is not one in a thousand of these human souls that cares to think, for ten minutes of the day, where this estate is or how beautiful it is, or what kind of life they are to lead in it, or what kind of life they must lead to obtain it.

You fancy that you care to know this: so little do you care that, probably, at this moment many of you are displeased with me for talking of the matter! You came to hear about the Art of this world, not about the Life of the next, and you are provoked with me for talking of what you can hear any Sunday in church. But do not be afraid. I will tell you something before you go about pictures, and carvings, and pottery, and what else you would like better to hear of than the other world. Nay, perhaps you say, "We want you to talk of pictures and pottery, because we are sure that you know something of them, and you know nothing of the other world. " Well— I don't. That is quite true. But the very strangeness and mystery of which I urge you to take notice, is in this—that I do not; —nor you either. Can you answer a single bold question unflinchingly about that other world? —Are you sure there is a heaven? Sure there is a hell? Sure that men are dropping before your faces through the pavements of these streets into eternal fire, or sure that they are not? Sure that at your own death you are going to be delivered from all sorrow, to be endowed with all virtue, to be gifted with all felicity, and raised into perpetual companionship with a King, compared to whom the kings of the earth are as grass-hoppers, and the nations as the dust of His feet? Are you sure of this? or, if not sure, do any of us so much as care to make it sure? and, if not, how can anything that we do be right—how can anything we think be wise? what honour can there be in the arts that amuse us, or what profit in the possessions that please?

Is not this a mystery of life?

But farther, you may, perhaps, think it a beneficent ordinance for the generality of men that they do not, with earnestness or anxiety, dwell on such questions of the future because the business of the day could not be done if this kind of thought were taken by all of us for the morrow. Be it so: but at least we might anticipate that the greatest and wisest of us, who were evidently the appointed teachers of the rest, would set themselves apart to seek out whatever could be surely known of the future destinies of their race; and to teach this in no rhetorical or ambiguous manner, but in the plainest and most severely earnest words.

Now, the highest representatives of men who have thus endeavoured, during the Christian era, to search out these deep things, and relate them, are Dante and Milton. There are none who for earnestness of thought, for mastery of word, can be classed with these. I am not at present, mind you, speaking of persons set apart in any priestly or pastoral office, to deliver creeds to us, or doctrines; but of men who try to discover and set forth, as far as by human intellect is possible, the facts of the other world. Divines may perhaps teach us how to arrive there, but only these two poets have in any powerful manner striven to discover, or in any definite words professed to tell, what we shall see and become there; or how those upper and nether worlds are, and have been, inhabited.

And what have they told us? Milton's account of the most important event in his whole system of the universe, the fall of the angels, is evidently unbelievable to himself; and the more so, that it is wholly founded on, and in a great part spoiled and degraded from, Hesiod's account of the decisive war of the younger gods with the Titans. The rest of his poem is a picturesque drama, in which every artifice of invention is visibly and consciously employed; not a single fact being, for an instant, conceived as tenable by any living faith. Dante's conception is far more intense, and, by himself, for the time, not to be escaped from; it is indeed a vision, but a vision only, and that one of the wildest that ever entranced a soul—a dream in which every grotesque type or phantasy of heathen tradition is renewed, and adorned; and the destinies of the Christian Church, under their most sacred symbols, become literally subordinate to the praise, and are only to be understood by the aid, of one dear Florentine maiden.

I tell you truly that, as I strive more with this strange lethargy and trance in myself, and awake to the meaning and power of life, it seems daily more amazing to me that men such as these should dare to play with the most precious truths, (or the most deadly untruths,) by which the whole human race listening to them could be informed, or deceived; —all the world their audiences for ever, with pleased ear, and passionate heart; —and yet, to this submissive infinitude of souls, and evermore succeeding and succeeding multitude, hungry for bread of life, they do but play upon sweetly modulated pipes; with pompous nomenclature adorn the councils of hell; touch a troubadour's guitar to the courses of the suns; and fill the openings of eternity, before which prophets have veiled their faces, and which angels desire to look into, with idle puppets of their scholastic imagination, and melancholy lights of frantic faith in their lost mortal love.

Is not this a mystery of life?

But more. We have to remember that these two great teachers were both of them warped in their temper, and thwarted in their search for truth. They were men of intellectual war, unable, through darkness of controversy, or stress of personal grief, to discern where their own ambition modified their utterances of the moral law; or their own agony mingled with their anger at its violation. But greater men than these have been—innocent-hearted—too great for contest. Men, like Homer and Shakespeare, of so unrecognised personality, that it disappears in future ages, and becomes ghostly, like the tradition of a lost heathen god. Men, therefore, to whose unoffended, uncondemning sight, the whole of human nature reveals itself in a pathetic weakness, with which they will not strive; or in mournful and transitory strength, which they dare not praise. And all Pagan and Christian Civilization thus becomes subject to them. It does not matter how little, or how much, any of us have read, either of Homer or Shakespeare; everything round us, in substance, or in thought, has been moulded by them. All Greek gentlemen were educated under Homer. All Roman gentlemen, by Greek literature. All Italian, and French, and English gentlemen, by Roman literature, and by its principles. Of the scope of Shakespeare, I will say only, that the intellectual measure of every man since born, in the domains of creative thought, may be assigned to him, according to the degree in which he has been taught by Shakespeare. Well, what do these two men, centres of mortal intelligence, deliver to us of conviction respecting what it most behoves that intelligence to grasp? What is their hope—their crown of rejoicing? what manner of exhortation have they for us, or of rebuke? what lies next their own hearts, and dictates their undying words? Have they any peace to promise to our unrest—any redemption to our misery?

Take Homer first, and think if there is any sadder image of human fate than the great Homeric story. The main features in the character of Achilles are its intense desire of justice, and its tenderness of affection. And in that bitter song of the Iliad, this man, though aided continually by the wisest of the gods, and burning with the desire of justice in his heart, becomes yet, through ill- governed passion, the most unjust of men: and, full of the deepest tenderness in his heart, becomes yet, through ill-governed passion, the most cruel of men. Intense alike in love and in friendship, he loses, first his mistress, and then his friend; for the sake of the one, he surrenders to death the armies of his own land; for the sake of the other, he surrenders all. Will a man lay down his life for his friend? Yea—even for his DEAD friend, this Achilles, though goddess-born, and goddess-taught, gives up his kingdom, his country, and his life—casts alike the innocent and guilty, with himself, into one gulf of slaughter, and dies at last by the hand of the basest of his adversaries.

Is not this a mystery of life?

But what, then, is the message to us of our own poet, and searcher of hearts, after fifteen hundred years of Christian faith have been numbered over the graves of men? Are his words more cheerful than the Heathen's—is his hope more near—his trust more sure—his reading of fate more happy? Ah, no! He differs from the Heathen poet chiefly in this—that he recognizes, for deliverance, no gods nigh at hand; and that, by petty chance—by momentary folly—by broken message—by fool's tyranny—or traitor's snare, the strongest and most righteous are brought to their ruin, and perish without word of hope. He indeed, as part of his rendering of character, ascribes the power and modesty of habitual devotion to the gentle and the just. The death-bed of Katharine is bright with visions of angels; and the great soldier-king, standing by his few dead, acknowledges the presence of the Hand that can save alike by many or by few. But observe that from those who with deepest spirit, meditate, and with deepest passion, mourn, there are no such words as these; nor in their hearts are any such consolations. Instead of the perpetual sense of the helpful presence of the Deity, which, through all heathen tradition, is the source of heroic strength, in battle, in exile, and in the valley of the shadow of death, we find only in the great Christian poet, the consciousness of a moral law, through which "the gods are just, and of our pleasant vices make instruments to scourge us; " and of the resolved arbitration of the destinies, that conclude into precision of doom what we feebly and blindly began; and force us, when our indiscretion serves us, and our deepest plots do pall, to the confession, that "there's a divinity that shapes our ends, rough hew them how we will. "

Is not this a mystery of life?

Be it so, then. About this human life that is to be, or that is, the wise religious men tell us nothing that we can trust; and the wise contemplative men, nothing that can give us peace. But there is yet a third class, to whom we may turn—the wise practical men. We have sat at the feet of the poets who sang of heaven, and they have told us their dreams. We have listened to the poets who sang of earth, and they have chanted to us dirges and words of despair. But there is one class of men more: - men, not capable of vision, nor sensitive to sorrow, but firm of purpose—practised in business; learned in all that can be, (by handling,) known. Men, whose hearts and hopes are wholly in this present world, from whom, therefore, we may surely learn, at least, how, at present, conveniently to live in it. What will THEY say to us, or show us by example? These kings— these councillors—these statesmen and builders of kingdoms—these capitalists and men of business, who weigh the earth, and the dust of it, in a balance. They know the world, surely; and what is the mystery of life to us, is none to them. They can surely show us how to live, while we live, and to gather out of the present world what is best.

I think I can best tell you their answer, by telling you a dream I had once. For though I am no poet, I have dreams sometimes: - I dreamed I was at a child's Mayday party, in which every means of entertainment had been provided for them, by a wise and kind host. It was in a stately house, with beautiful gardens attached to it; and the children had been set free in the rooms and gardens, with no care whatever but how to pass their afternoon rejoicingly. They did not, indeed, know much about what was to happen next day; and some of them, I thought, were a little frightened, because there was a chance of their being sent to a new school where there were examinations; but they kept the thoughts of that out of their heads as well as they could, and resolved to enjoy themselves. The house, I said, was in a beautiful garden, and in the garden were all kinds of flowers; sweet, grassy banks for rest; and smooth lawns for play; and pleasant streams and woods; and rocky places for climbing. And the children were happy for a little while, but presently they separated themselves into parties; and then each party declared it would have a piece of the garden for its own, and that none of the others should have anything to do with that piece. Next, they quarrelled violently which pieces they would have; and at last the boys took up the thing, as boys should do, "practically, " and fought in the flower-beds till there was hardly a flower left standing; then they trampled down each other's bits of the garden out of spite; and the girls cried till they could cry no more; and so they all lay down at last breathless in the ruin, and waited for the time when they were to be taken home in the evening. {30}

Meanwhile, the children in the house had been making themselves happy also in their manner. For them, there had been provided every kind of indoor pleasure: there was music for them to dance to; and the library was open, with all manner of amusing books; and there was a museum full of the most curious shells, and animals, and birds; and there was a workshop, with lathes and carpenter's tools, for the ingenious boys; and there were pretty fantastic dresses, for the girls to dress in; and there were microscopes, and kaleidoscopes; and whatever toys a child could fancy; and a table, in the dining-room, loaded with everything nice to eat.

But, in the midst of all this, it struck two or three of the more "practical" children, that they would like some of the brass-headed nails that studded the chairs; and so they set to work to pull them out. Presently, the others, who were reading, or looking at shells, took a fancy to do the like; and, in a little while, all the children, nearly, were spraining their fingers, in pulling out brass-headed nails. With all that they could pull out, they were not satisfied; and then, everybody wanted some of somebody else's. And at last, the really practical and sensible ones declared, that nothing was of any real consequence, that afternoon, except to get plenty of brass-headed nails; and that the books, and the cakes, and the microscopes were of no use at all in themselves, but only, if they could be exchanged for nail-heads. And at last they began to fight for nail-heads, as the others fought for the bits of garden. Only here and there, a despised one shrank away into a corner, and tried to get a little quiet with a book, in the midst of the noise; but all the practical ones thought of nothing else but counting nail-heads all the afternoon—even though they knew they would not be allowed to carry so much as one brass knob away with them. But no—it was—"Who has most nails? I have a hundred, and you have fifty; or, I have a thousand, and you have two. I must have as many as you before I leave the house, or I cannot possibly go home in peace. " At last, they made so much noise that I awoke, and thought to myself,

"What a false dream that is, of CHILDREN! " The child is the father of the man; and wiser. Children never do such foolish things. Only men do.

But there is yet one last class of persons to be interrogated. The wise religious men we have asked in vain; the wise contemplative men, in vain; the wise worldly men, in vain. But there is another group yet. In the midst of this vanity of empty religion—of tragic contemplation—of wrathful and wretched ambition, and dispute for dust, there is yet one great group of persons, by whom all these disputers live—the persons who have determined, or have had it by a beneficent Providence determined for them, that they will do something useful; that whatever may be prepared for them hereafter, or happen to them here, they will, at least, deserve the food that God gives them by winning it honourably: and that, however fallen from the purity, or far from the peace, of Eden, they will carry out the duty of human dominion, though they have lost its felicity; and dress and keep the wilderness, though they no more can dress or keep the garden.

These, —hewers of wood, and drawers of water, —these, bent under burdens, or torn of scourges—these, that dig and weave—that plant and build; workers in wood, and in marble, and in iron—by whom all food, clothing, habitation, furniture, and means of delight are produced, for themselves, and for all men beside; men, whose deeds are good, though their words may be few; men, whose lives are serviceable, be they never so short, and worthy of honour, be they never so humble; —from these, surely, at least, we may receive some clear message of teaching; and pierce, for an instant, into the mystery of life, and of its arts.

Yes; from these, at last, we do receive a lesson. But I grieve to say, or rather—for that is the deeper truth of the matter—I rejoice to say—this message of theirs can only be received by joining them—not by thinking about them.

You sent for me to talk to you of art; and I have obeyed you in coming. But the main thing I have to tell you is, —that art must not be talked about. The fact that there is talk about it at all, signifies that it is ill done, or cannot be done. No true painter ever speaks, or ever has spoken, much of his art. The greatest speak nothing. Even Reynolds is no exception, for he wrote of all that he could not himself do, and was utterly silent respecting all that he himself did.

The moment a man can really do his work he becomes speechless about it. All words become idle to him—all theories.

Does a bird need to theorize about building its nest, or boast of it when built? All good work is essentially done that way—without hesitation, without difficulty, without boasting; and in the doers of the best, there is an inner and involuntary power which approximates literally to the instinct of an animal—nay, I am certain that in the most perfect human artists, reason does NOT supersede instinct, but is added to an instinct as much more divine than that of the lower animals as the human body is more beautiful than theirs; that a great singer sings not with less instinct than the nightingale, but with more—only more various, applicable, and governable; that a great architect does not build with less instinct than the beaver or the bee, but with more—with an innate cunning of proportion that embraces all beauty, and a divine ingenuity of skill that improvises all construction. But be that as it may—be the instinct less or more than that of inferior animals—like or unlike theirs, still the human art is dependent on that first, and then upon an amount of practice, of science, —and of imagination disciplined by thought, which the true possessor of it knows to be incommunicable, and the true critic of it, inexplicable, except through long process of laborious' years. That journey of life's conquest, in which hills over hills, and Alps on Alps arose, and sank, —do you think you can make another trace it painlessly, by talking? Why, you cannot even carry us up an Alp, by talking. You can guide us up it, step by step, no otherwise—even so, best silently. You girls, who have been among the hills, know how the bad guide chatters and gesticulates, and it is "Put your foot here; " and "Mind how you balance yourself there; " but the good guide walks on quietly, without a word, only with his eyes on you when need is, and his arm like an iron bar, if need be.

In that slow way, also, art can be taught—if you have faith in your guide, and will let his arm be to you as an iron bar when need is. But in what teacher of art have you such faith? Certainly not in me; for, as I told you at first, I know well enough it is only because you think I can talk, not because you think I know my business, that you let me speak to you at all. If I were to tell you anything that seemed to you strange you would not believe it, and yet it would only be in telling you strange things that I could be of use to you. I could be of great use to you—infinite use— with brief saying, if you would believe it; but you would not, just because the thing that would be of real use would displease you. You are all wild, for instance, with admiration of Gustave Dore. Well, suppose I were to tell you, in the strongest terms I could use, that Gustave Dore's art was bad—bad, not in weakness, —not in failure, —but bad with dreadful power—the power of the Furies and the Harpies mingled, enraging, and polluting; that so long as you looked at it, no perception of pure or beautiful art was possible for you. Suppose I were to tell you that! What would be the use? Would you look at Gustave Dore less? Rather, more, I fancy. On the other hand, I could soon put you into good humour with me, if I chose. I know well enough what you like, and how to praise it to your better liking. I could talk to you about moonlight, and twilight, and spring flowers, and autumn leaves, and the Madonnas of Raphael—how motherly! and the Sibyls of Michael Angelo—how majestic! and the Saints of Angelico—how pious! and the Cherubs of Correggio—how delicious! Old as I am, I could play you a tune on the harp yet, that you would dance to. But neither you nor I should be a bit the better or wiser; or, if we were, our increased wisdom could be of no practical effect. For, indeed, the arts, as regards teachableness, differ from the sciences also in this, that their power is founded not merely on facts which can be communicated, but on dispositions which require to be created. Art is neither to be achieved by effort of thinking, nor explained by accuracy of speaking. It is the instinctive and necessary result of power, which can only be developed through the mind of successive generations, and which finally burst into life under social conditions as slow of growth as the faculties they regulate. Whole aeras of mighty history are summed, and the passions of dead myriads are concentrated, in the existence of a noble art, and if that noble art were among us, we should feel it and rejoice; not caring in the least to hear lectures on it; and since it is not among us, be assured we have to go back to the root of it, or, at least, to the place where the stock of it is yet alive, and the branches began to die.

And now, may I have your pardon for pointing out, partly with reference to matters which are at this time of greater moment than the arts—that if we undertook such recession to the vital germ of national arts that have decayed, we should find a more singular arrest of their power in Ireland than in any other European country? For in the eighth century Ireland possessed a school of art in her manuscripts and sculpture, which, in many of its qualities—apparently in all essential qualities of decorative invention—was quite without rival; seeming as if it might have advanced to the highest triumphs in architecture and in painting. But there was one fatal flaw in its nature, by which it was stayed, and stayed with a conspicuousness of pause to which there is no parallel: so that, long ago, in tracing the progress of European schools from infancy to strength, I chose for the students of Kensington, in a lecture since published, two characteristic examples of early art, of equal skill; but in the one case, skill which was progressive—in the other, skill which was at pause. In the one case, it was work receptive of correction—hungry for correction; and in the other, work which inherently rejected correction. I chose for them a corrigible Eve, and an incorrigible Angel, and I grieve to say that the incorrigible Angel was also an Irish Angel! {31}

And the fatal difference lay wholly in this. In both pieces of art there was an equal falling short of the needs of fact; but the Lombardic Eve knew she was in the wrong, and the Irish Angel thought himself all right. The eager Lombardic sculptor, though firmly insisting on his childish idea, yet showed in the irregular broken touches of the features, and the imperfect struggle for softer lines in the form, a perception of beauty and law that he could not render; there was the strain of effort, under conscious imperfection, in every line. But the Irish missal-painter had drawn his angel with no sense of failure, in happy complacency, and put red dots into the palm of each hand, and rounded the eyes into perfect circles, and, I regret to say, left the mouth out altogether, with perfect satisfaction to himself.

May I without offence ask you to consider whether this mode of arrest in ancient Irish art may not be indicative of points of character which even yet, in some measure, arrest your national power? I have seen much of Irish character, and have watched it closely, for I have also much loved it. And I think the form of failure to which it is most liable is this, —that being generous- hearted, and wholly intending always to do right, it does not attend to the external laws of right, but thinks it must necessarily do right because it means to do so, and therefore does wrong without finding it out; and then, when the consequences of its wrong come upon it, or upon others connected with it, it cannot conceive that the wrong is in anywise of its causing or of its doing, but flies into wrath, and a strange agony of desire for justice, as feeling itself wholly innocent, which leads it farther astray, until there is nothing that it is not capable of doing with a good conscience.

But mind, I do not mean to say that, in past or present relations between Ireland and England, you have been wrong, and we right. Far from that, I believe that in all great questions of principle, and in all details of administration of law, you have been usually right, and we wrong; sometimes in misunderstanding you, sometimes in resolute iniquity to you. Nevertheless, in all disputes between states, though the stronger is nearly always mainly in the wrong, the weaker is often so in a minor degree; and I think we sometimes admit the possibility of our being in error, and you never do.

And now, returning to the broader question, what these arts and labours of life have to teach us of its mystery, this is the first of their lessons—that the more beautiful the art, the more it is essentially the work of people who FEEL THEMSELVES WRONG; —who are striving for the fulfilment of a law, and the grasp of a loveliness, which they have not yet attained, which they feel even farther and farther from attaining the more they strive for it. And yet, in still deeper sense, it is the work of people who know also that they are right. The very sense of inevitable error from their purpose marks the perfectness of that purpose, and the continued sense of failure arises from the continued opening of the eyes more clearly to all the sacredest laws of truth.

This is one lesson. The second is a very plain, and greatly precious one: namely—that whenever the arts and labours of life are fulfilled in this spirit of striving against misrule, and doing whatever we have to do, honourably and perfectly, they invariably bring happiness, as much as seems possible to the nature of man. In all other paths by which that happiness is pursued there is disappointment, or destruction: for ambition and for passion there is no rest—no fruition; the fairest pleasures of youth perish in a darkness greater than their past light: and the loftiest and purest love too often does but inflame the cloud of life with endless fire of pain. But, ascending from lowest to highest, through every scale of human industry, that industry worthily followed, gives peace. Ask the labourer in the field, at the forge, or in the mine; ask the patient, delicate-fingered artisan, or the strong-armed, fiery- hearted worker in bronze, and in marble, and with the colours of light; and none of these, who are true workmen, will ever tell you, that they have found the law of heaven an unkind one—that in the sweat of their face they should eat bread, till they return to the ground; nor that they ever found it an unrewarded obedience, if, indeed, it was rendered faithfully to the command—"Whatsoever thy hand findeth to do—do it with thy might. "

These are the two great and constant lessons which our labourers teach us of the mystery of life. But there is another, and a sadder one, which they cannot teach us, which we must read on their tombstones.

"Do it with thy might. " There have been myriads upon myriads of human creatures who have obeyed this law—who have put every breath and nerve of their being into its toil—who have devoted every hour, and exhausted every faculty—who have bequeathed their unaccomplished thoughts at death—who, being dead, have yet spoken, by majesty of memory, and strength of example. And, at last, what has all this "Might" of humanity accomplished, in six thousand years of labour and sorrow? What has it DONE? Take the three chief occupations and arts of men, one by one, and count their achievements. Begin with the first—the lord of them all—Agriculture. Six thousand years have passed since we were set to till the ground, from which we were taken. How much of it is tilled? How much of that which is, wisely or well? In the very centre and chief garden of Europe—where the two forms of parent Christianity have had their fortresses—where the noble Catholics of the Forest Cantons, and the noble Protestants of the Vaudois valleys, have maintained, for dateless ages, their faiths and liberties—there the unchecked Alpine rivers yet run wild in devastation; and the marshes, which a few hundred men could redeem with a year's labour, still blast their helpless inhabitants into fevered idiotism. That is so, in the centre of Europe! While, on the near coast of Africa, once the Garden of the Hesperides, an Arab woman, but a few sunsets since, ate her child, for famine. And, with all the treasures of the East at our feet, we, in our own dominion, could not find a few grains of rice, for a people that asked of us no more; but stood by, and saw five hundred thousand of them perish of hunger.

Then, after agriculture, the art of kings, take the next head of human arts—Weaving; the art of queens, honoured of all noble Heathen women, in the person of their virgin goddess—honoured of all Hebrew women, by the word of their wisest king—"She layeth her hands to the spindle, and her hands hold the distaff; she stretcheth out her hand to the poor. She is not afraid of the snow for her household, for all her household are clothed with scarlet. She maketh herself covering of tapestry; her clothing is silk and purple. She maketh fine linen, and selleth it, and delivereth girdles to the merchant. " What have we done in all these thousands of years with this bright art of Greek maid and Christian matron? Six thousand years of weaving, and have we learned to weave? Might not every naked wall have been purple with tapestry, and every feeble breast fenced with sweet colours from the cold? What have we done? Our fingers are too few, it seems, to twist together some poor covering for our bodies. We set our streams to work for us, and choke the air with fire, to turn our spinning-wheels—and, —ARE WE YET CLOTHED? Are not the streets of the capitals of Europe foul with sale of cast clouts and rotten rags? Is not the beauty of your sweet children left in wretchedness of disgrace, while, with better honour, nature clothes the brood of the bird in its nest, and the suckling of the wolf in her den? And does not every winter's snow robe what you have not robed, and shroud what you have not shrouded; and every winter's wind bear up to heaven its wasted souls, to witness against you hereafter, by the voice of their Christ, —"I was naked, and ye clothed me not"?

Lastly—take the Art of Building—the strongest—proudest—most orderly—most enduring of the arts of man; that of which the produce is in the surest manner accumulative, and need not perish, or be replaced; but if once well done, will stand more strongly than the unbalanced rocks—more prevalently than the crumbling hills. The art which is associated with all civic pride and sacred principle; with which men record their power—satisfy their enthusiasm—make sure their defence—define and make dear their habitation. And in six thousand years of building, what have we done? Of the greater part of all that skill and strength, NO vestige is left, but fallen stones, that encumber the fields and impede the streams. But, from this waste of disorder, and of time, and of rage, what IS left to us? Constructive and progressive creatures, that we are, with ruling brains, and forming hands, capable of fellowship, and thirsting for fame, can we not contend, in comfort, with the insects of the forest, or, in achievement, with the worm of the sea? The white surf rages in vain against the ramparts built by poor atoms of scarcely nascent life; but only ridges of formless ruin mark the places where once dwelt our noblest multitudes. The ant and the moth have cells for each of their young, but our little ones lie in festering heaps, in homes that consume them like graves; and night by night, from the corners of our streets, rises up the cry of the homeless—"I was a stranger, and ye took me not in. "

Must it be always thus? Is our life for ever to be without profit—without possession? Shall the strength of its generations be as barren as death; or cast away their labour, as the wild fig-tree casts her untimely figs? Is it all a dream then—the desire of the eyes and the pride of life—or, if it be, might we not live in nobler dream than this? The poets and prophets, the wise men, and the scribes, though they have told us nothing about a life to come, have told us much about the life that is now. They have had—they also, —their dreams, and we have laughed at them. They have dreamed of mercy, and of justice; they have dreamed of peace and good-will; they have dreamed of labour undisappointed, and of rest undisturbed; they have dreamed of fulness in harvest, and overflowing in store; they have dreamed of wisdom in council, and of providence in law; of gladness of parents, and strength of children, and glory of grey hairs. And at these visions of theirs we have mocked, and held them for idle and vain, unreal and unaccomplishable. What have we accomplished with our realities? Is this what has come of our worldly wisdom, tried against their folly? this, our mightiest possible, against their impotent ideal? or, have we only wandered among the spectra of a baser felicity, and chased phantoms of the tombs, instead of visions of the Almighty; and walked after the imaginations of our evil hearts, instead of after the counsels of Eternity, until our lives—not in the likeness of the cloud of heaven, but of the smoke of hell—have become "as a vapour, that appeareth for a little time, and then vanisheth away"?

DOES it vanish then? Are you sure of that? —sure, that the nothingness of the grave will be a rest from this troubled nothingness; and that the coiling shadow, which disquiets itself in vain, cannot change into the smoke of the torment that ascends for ever? Will any answer that they ARE sure of it, and that there is no fear, nor hope, nor desire, nor labour, whither they go? Be it so: will you not, then, make as sure of the Life that now is, as you are of the Death that is to come? Your hearts are wholly in this world—will you not give them to it wisely, as well as perfectly? And see, first of all, that you HAVE hearts, and sound hearts, too, to give. Because you have no heaven to look for, is that any reason that you should remain ignorant of this wonderful and infinite earth, which is firmly and instantly given you in possession? Although your days are numbered, and the following darkness sure, is it necessary that you should share the degradation of the brute, because you are condemned to its mortality; or live the life of the moth, and of the worm, because you are to companion them in the dust? Not so; we may have but a few thousands of days to spend, perhaps hundreds only—perhaps tens; nay, the longest of our time and best, looked back on, will be but as a moment, as the twinkling of an eye; still we are men, not insects; we are living spirits, not passing clouds. "He maketh the winds His messengers; the momentary fire, His minister; " and shall we do less than THESE? Let us do the work of men while we bear the form of them; and, as we snatch our narrow portion of time out of Eternity, snatch also our narrow inheritance of passion out of Immortality—even though our lives BE as a vapour, that appeareth for a little time, and then vanisheth away.

But there are some of you who believe not this—who think this cloud of life has no such close—that it is to float, revealed and illumined, upon the floor of heaven, in the day when He cometh with clouds, and every eye shall see Him. Some day, you believe, within these five, or ten, or twenty years, for every one of us the judgment will be set, and the books opened. If that be true, far more than that must be true. Is there but one day of judgment? Why, for us every day is a day of judgment—every day is a Dies Irae, and writes its irrevocable verdict in the flame of its West. Think you that judgment waits till the doors of the grave are opened? It waits at the doors of your houses—it waits at the corners of your streets; we are in the midst of judgment—the insects that we crush are our judges—the moments we fret away are our judges—the elements that feed us, judge, as they minister—and the pleasures that deceive us, judge, as they indulge. Let us, for our lives, do the work of Men while we bear the form of them, if indeed those lives are NOT as a vapour, and do NOT vanish away.

"The work of men"—and what is that? Well, we may any of us know very quickly, on the condition of being wholly ready to do it. But many of us are for the most part thinking, not of what we are to do, but of what we are to get; and the best of us are sunk into the sin of Ananias, and it is a mortal one—we want to keep back part of the price; and we continually talk of taking up our cross, as if the only harm in a cross was the WEIGHT of it—as if it was only a thing to be carried, instead of to be—crucified upon. "They that are His have crucified the flesh, with the affections and lusts. " Does that mean, think you, that in time of national distress, of religious trial, of crisis for every interest and hope of humanity—none of us will cease jesting, none cease idling, none put themselves to any wholesome work, none take so much as a tag of lace off their footmen's coats, to save the world? Or does it rather mean, that they are ready to leave houses, lands, and kindreds—yes, and life, if need be? Life! —some of us are ready enough to throw that away, joyless as we have made it. But "STATION in Life"—how many of us are ready to quit

THAT? Is it not always the great objection, where there is question of finding something useful to do—"We cannot leave our stations in Life"?

Those of us who really cannot—that is to say, who can only maintain themselves by continuing in some business or salaried office, have already something to do; and all that they have to see to is, that they do it honestly and with all their might. But with most people who use that apology, "remaining in the station of life to which Providence has called them" means keeping all the carriages, and all the footmen and large houses they can possibly pay for; and, once for all, I say that if ever Providence DID put them into stations of that sort—which is not at all a matter of certainty—Providence is just now very distinctly calling them out again. Levi's station in life was the receipt of custom; and Peter's, the shore of Galilee; and Paul's, the antechambers of the High Priest, —which "station in life" each had to leave, with brief notice.

And, whatever our station in life may be, at this crisis, those of us who mean to fulfil our duty ought first to live on as little as we can; and, secondly, to do all the wholesome work for it we can, and to spend all we can spare in doing all the sure good we can.

And sure good is, first in feeding people, then in dressing people, then in lodging people, and lastly in rightly pleasing people, with arts, or sciences, or any other subject of thought.

I say first in feeding; and, once for all, do not let yourselves be deceived by any of the common talk of "indiscriminate charity. " The order to us is not to feed the deserving hungry, nor the industrious hungry, nor the amiable and well-intentioned hungry, but simply to feed the hungry. It is quite true, infallibly true, that if any man will not work, neither should he eat—think of that, and every time you sit down to your dinner, ladies and gentlemen, say solemnly, before you ask a blessing, "How much work have I done to-day for my dinner? " But the proper way to enforce that order on those below you, as well as on yourselves, is not to leave vagabonds and honest people to starve together, but very distinctly to discern and seize your vagabond; and shut your vagabond up out of honest people's way, and very sternly then see that, until he has worked, he does NOT eat. But the first thing is to be sure you have the food to give; and, therefore, to enforce the organization of vast activities in agriculture and in commerce, for the production of the wholesomest food, and proper storing and distribution of it, so that no famine shall any more be possible among civilized beings. There is plenty of work in this business alone, and at once, for any number of people who like to engage in it.

Secondly, dressing people—that is to say, urging every one, within reach of your influence to be always neat and clean, and giving them means of being so. In so far as they absolutely refuse, you must give up the effort with respect to them, only taking care that no children within your sphere of influence shall any more be brought up with such habits; and that every person who is willing to dress with propriety shall have encouragement to do so. And the first absolutely necessary step towards this is the gradual adoption of a consistent dress for different ranks of persons, so that their rank shall be known by their dress; and the restriction of the changes of fashion within certain limits. All which appears for the present quite impossible; but it is only so far even difficult as it is difficult to conquer our vanity, frivolity, and desire to appear what we are not. And it is not, nor ever shall be, creed of mine, that these mean and shallow vices are unconquerable by Christian women.

And then, thirdly, lodging people, which you may think should have been put first, but I put it third, because we must feed and clothe people where we find them, and lodge them afterwards. And providing lodgment for them means a great deal of vigorous legislature, and cutting down of vested interests that stand in the way, and after that, or before that, so far as we can get it, thorough sanitary and remedial action in the houses that we have; and then the building of more, strongly, beautifully, and in groups of limited extent, kept in proportion to their streams, and walled round, so that there may be no festering and wretched suburb anywhere, but clean and busy street within, and the open country without, with a belt of beautiful garden and orchard round the walls, so that from any part of the city perfectly fresh air and grass, and sight of far horizon, might be reachable in a few minutes' walk. This the final aim; but in immediate action every minor and possible good to be instantly done, when, and as, we can; roofs mended that have holes in them—fences patched that have gaps in them—walls' buttressed that totter—and floors propped that shake; cleanliness and order enforced with our own hands and eyes, till we are breathless, every day. And all the fine arts will healthily follow. I myself have washed a flight of stone stairs all down, with bucket and broom, in a Savoy inn, where they hadn't washed their stairs since they first went up them; and I never made a better sketch than that afternoon.

These, then, are the three first needs of civilized life; and the law for every Christian man and woman is, that they shall be in direct service towards one of these three needs, as far as is consistent with their own special occupation, and if they have no special business, then wholly in one of these services. And out of such exertion in plain duty all other good will come; for in this direct contention with material evil, you will find out the real nature of all evil; you will discern by the various kinds of resistance, what is really the fault and main antagonism to good; also you will find the most unexpected helps and profound lessons given, and truths will come thus down to us which the speculation of all our lives would never have raised us up to. You will find nearly every educational problem solved, as soon as you truly want to do something; everybody will become of use in their own fittest way, and will learn what is best for them to know in that use. Competitive examination will then, and not till then, be wholesome, because it will be daily, and calm, and in practice; and on these familiar arts, and minute, but certain and serviceable knowledges, will be surely edified and sustained the greater arts and splendid theoretical sciences.

But much more than this. On such holy and simple practice will be founded, indeed, at last, an infallible religion. The greatest of all the mysteries of life, and the most terrible, is the corruption of even the sincerest religion, which is not daily founded on rational, effective, humble, and helpful action. Helpful action, observe! for there is just one law, which, obeyed, keeps all religions pure—forgotten, makes them all false. Whenever in any religious faith, dark or bright, we allow our minds to dwell upon the points in which we differ from other people, we are wrong, and in the devil's power. That is the essence of the Pharisee's thanksgiving—"Lord, I thank Thee that I am not as other men are. " At every moment of our lives we should be trying to find out, not in what we differ from other people, but in what we agree with them; and the moment we find we can agree as to anything that should be done, kind or good, (and who but fools couldn't?) then do it; push at it together: you can't quarrel in a side-by-side push; but the moment that even the best men stop pushing, and begin talking, they mistake their pugnacity for piety, and it's all over. I will not speak of the crimes which in past times have been committed in the name of Christ, nor of the follies which are at this hour held to be consistent with obedience to Him; but I WILL speak of the morbid corruption and waste of vital power in religious sentiment, by which the pure strength of that which should be the guiding soul of every nation, the splendour of its youthful manhood, and spotless light of its maidenhood, is averted or cast away. You may see continually girls who have never been taught to do a single useful thing thoroughly; who cannot sew, who cannot cook, who cannot cast an account, nor prepare a medicine, whose whole life has been passed either in play or in pride; you will find girls like these, when they are earnest-hearted, cast all their innate passion of religious spirit, which was meant by God to support them through the irksomeness of daily toil, into grievous and vain meditation over the meaning of the great Book, of which no syllable was ever yet to be understood but through a deed; all the instinctive wisdom and mercy of their womanhood made vain, and the glory of their pure consciences warped into fruitless agony concerning questions which the laws of common serviceable life would have either solved for them in an instant, or kept out of their way. Give such a girl any true work that will make her active in the dawn, and weary at night, with the consciousness that her fellow-creatures have indeed been the better for her day, and the powerless sorrow of her enthusiasm will transform itself into a majesty of radiant and beneficent peace.

So with our youths. We once taught them to make Latin verses, and called them educated; now we teach them to leap and to row, to hit a ball with a bat, and call them educated. Can they plough, can they sow, can they plant at the right time, or build with a steady hand? Is it the effort of their lives to be chaste, knightly, faithful, holy in thought, lovely in word and deed? Indeed it is, with some, nay, with many, and the strength of England is in them, and the hope; but we have to turn their courage from the toil of war to the toil of mercy; and their intellect from dispute of words to discernment of things; and their knighthood from the errantry of adventure to the state and fidelity of a kingly power. And then, indeed, shall abide, for them and for us, an incorruptible felicity, and an infallible religion; shall abide for us Faith, no more to be assailed by temptation, no more to be defended by wrath and by fear; —shall abide with us Hope, no more to be quenched by the years that overwhelm, or made ashamed by the shadows that betray: - shall abide for us, and with us, the greatest of these; the abiding will, the abiding name of our Father. For the greatest of these is Charity.

Footnotes:

{1} The paragraph that begins "I think I can best tell you their answer... "

{2} The paragraph that begins "Does a bird... "

{3} The paragraphs beginning:

79—"I believe, then, with this exception... " 75—"Yet, observe, with exquisite accuracy... " 19—"Now, in order to deal with words rightly,... " 79—"Then, in art, keep the finest models... "

{4} [Greek word which cannot be reproduced]

{5} Note this sentence carefully, and compare the 'Queen of the Air, ' paragraph "Nothing that I ever said is more... "

{6} 2 Peter iii. 5-7.

{7} Compare the 13th Letter in 'Time and Tide. '

{8} Modern "Education" for the most part signifies giving people the faculty of thinking wrong on every conceivable subject of importance to them.

{9} Inf. xxiii. 125, 126; xix. 49. 50.

{10} Compare with paragraph "This, then, is what you have to do... "

{11} See note at end of lecture. I have put it in large type, because the course of matters since it was written has made it perhaps better worth attention.

{12} Respecting the increase of rent by the deaths of the poor, for evidence of which see the preface to the Medical Officer's report to the Privy Council, just published, there are suggestions in its preface which will make some stir among us, I fancy, respecting which let me note these points following: -

There are two theories on the subject of land now abroad, and in contention; both false.

The first is that, by Heavenly law, there have always existed, and must continue to exist, a certain number of hereditarily sacred persons to whom the earth, air, and water of the world belong, as personal property; of which earth, air, and water, these persons may, at their pleasure, permit, or forbid, the rest of the human race to eat, to breathe, or to drink. This theory is not for many years longer tenable. The adverse theory is that a division of the land of the world among the mob of the world would immediately elevate the said mob into sacred personages; that houses would then build themselves, and corn grow of itself; and that everybody would be able to live, without doing any work for his living. This theory would also be found highly untenable in practice.

It will, however, require some rough experiments and rougher catastrophes, before the generality of persons will be convinced that no law concerning anything—least of all concerning land, for either holding or dividing it, or renting it high, or renting it low—would be of the smallest ultimate use to the people, so long as the general contest for life, and for the means of life, remains one of mere brutal competition. That contest, in an unprincipled nation, will take one deadly form or another, whatever laws you make against it. For instance, it would be an entirely wholesome law for England, if it could be carried, that maximum limits should be assigned to incomes according to classes; and that every nobleman's income should be paid to him as a fixed salary or pension by the nation; and not squeezed by him in variable sums, at discretion, out of the tenants of his land. But if you could get such a law passed to-morrow, and if, which would be farther necessary, you could fix the value of the assigned incomes by making a given weight of pure bread for a given sum, a twelvemonth would not pass before another currency would have been tacitly established, and the power of accumulated wealth would have re-asserted itself in some other article, or some other imaginary sign. There is only one cure for public distress—and that is public education, directed to make men thoughtful, merciful, and just. There are, indeed, many laws conceivable which would gradually better and strengthen the national temper; but, for the most part, they are such as the national temper must be much bettered before it would bear. A nation in its youth may be helped by laws, as a weak child by backboards, but when it is old it cannot that way strengthen its crooked spine.

And besides; the problem of land, at its worst, is a bye one; distribute the earth as you will, the principal question remains inexorable, —

Who is to dig it? Which of us, in brief word, is to do the hard and dirty work for the rest, and for what pay? Who is to do the pleasant and clean work, and for what pay? Who is do no work, and for what pay? And there are curious moral and religious questions connected with these. How far is it lawful to suck a portion of the soul out of a great many persons, in order to put the abstracted psychical quantities together and make one very beautiful or ideal soul? If we had to deal with mere blood instead of spirit, (and the thing might literally be done—as it has been done with infants before now)—so that it were possible, by taking a certain quantity of blood from the arms of a given number of the mob, and putting it all into one person, to make a more azure-blooded gentleman of him, the thing would of course be managed; but secretly, I should conceive. But now, because it is brain and soul that we abstract, not visible blood, it can be done quite openly, and we live, we gentlemen, on delicatest prey, after the manner of weasels; that is to say, we keep a certain number of clowns digging and ditching, and generally stupefied, in order that we, being fed gratis, may have all the thinking and feeling to ourselves. Yet there is a great deal to be said for this. A highly-bred and trained English, French, Austrian, or Italian gentleman (much more a lady), is a great production, —a better production than most statues; being beautifully coloured as well as shaped, and plus all the brains; a glorious thing to look at, a wonderful thing to talk to; and you cannot have it, any more than a pyramid or a church, but by sacrifice of much contributed life. And it is, perhaps, better to build a beautiful human creature than a beautiful dome or steeple—and more delightful to look up reverently to a creature far above us, than to a wall; only the beautiful human creature will have some duties to do in return—duties of living belfry and rampart—of which presently.

{13} Since this was written, the answer has become definitely—No; we having surrendered the field of Arctic discovery to the Continental nations, as being ourselves too poor to pay for ships.

{14} I state this fact without Professor Owen's permission: which of course he could not with propriety have granted, had I asked it; but I consider it so important that the public should be aware of the fact, that I do what seems to me right, though rude.

{15} That was our real idea of "Free Trade" —"All the trade to myself. " You find now that by "competition" other people can manage to sell something as well as you—and now we call for Protection again. Wretches!

{16} I meant that the beautiful places of the world—Switzerland, Italy, South Germany, and so on—are, indeed, the truest cathedrals--places to be reverent in, and to worship in; and that we only care to drive through them: and to eat and drink at their most sacred places.

{17} I was singularly struck, some years ago, by finding all the river shore at Richmond, in Yorkshire, black in its earth, from the mere drift of soot-laden air from places many miles away.

{18} One of the things which we must very resolutely enforce, for the good of all classes, in our future arrangements, must be that they wear no "translated" articles of dress. See the preface.

{19} This abbreviation of the penalty of useless labour is curiously coincident in verbal form with a certain passage which some of us may remember. It may perhaps be well to preserve beside this paragraph another cutting out of my store-drawer, from the 'Morning Post, ' of about a parallel date, Friday, March 10th, 1865: - "The SALONS of Mme. C-, who did the honours with clever imitative grace and elegance, were crowded with princes, dukes, marquises, and counts—in fact, with the same MALE company as one meets at the parties of the Princess Metternich and Madame Drouyn de Lhuys. Some English peers and members of Parliament were present, and appeared to enjoy the animated and dazzlingly improper scene. On the second floor the supper tables were loaded with every delicacy of the season. That your readers may form some idea of the dainty fare of the Parisian demi-monde, I copy the menu of the supper, which was served to all the guests (about 200) seated at four o'clock. Choice Yquem, Johannisberg, Laffitte, Tokay, and champagne of the finest vintages were served most lavishly throughout the morning. After supper dancing was resumed with increased animation, and the ball terminated with a CHAINE DIABOLIQUE and a CANCAN D'ENFER at seven in the morning. (Morning service—'Ere the fresh lawns appeared, under the opening eyelids of the Morn. -') Here is the menu: - 'Consomme de volaille e la Bagration: 16 hors-d'oeuvres varies. Bouchees e la Talleyrand. Saumons froids, sauce Ravigote. Filets de boeuf en Bellevue, timbales milanaises, chaudfroid de gibier. Dindes truffees. Pates de foies gras, buissons d'ecrevisses, salades venetiennes, gelees blanches aux fruits, gateaux mancini, parisiens et parisiennes. Fromages glaces. Ananas. Dessert. '"

{20} Please observe this statement, and think of it, and consider how it happens that a poor old woman will be ashamed to take a shilling a week from the country—but no one is ashamed to take a pension of a thousand a year.

{21} I am heartily glad to see such a paper as the 'Pall Mall Gazette' established; for the power of the press in the hands of highly educated men, in independent position, and of honest purpose, may indeed become all that it has been hitherto vainly vaunted to be. Its editor will therefore, I doubt not, pardon me, in that, by very reason of my respect for the journal, I do not let pass unnoticed an article in its third number, page 5, which was wrong in every word of it, with the intense wrongness which only an honest man can achieve who has taken a false turn of thought in the outset, and is following it, regardless of consequences. It contained at the end this notable passage: -

"The bread of affliction, and the water of affliction, —aye, and the bedsteads and blankets of affliction, are the very utmost that the law ought to give to OUTCASTS MERELY AS OUTCASTS. " I merely put beside this expression of the gentlemanly mind of England in 1865, a part of the message which Isaiah was ordered to "lift up his voice like a trumpet" in declaring to the gentlemen of his day: "Ye fast for strife, and to smite with the fist of wickedness. Is not this the fast that I have chosen, to deal thy bread to the hungry, and that thou bring the poor THAT ARE CAST OUT (margin, 'afflicted') to THY house? " The falsehood on which the writer had mentally founded himself, as previously stated by him, was this: "To confound the functions of the dispensers of the poor-rates with those of the dispensers of a charitable institution is a great and pernicious error. " This sentence is so accurately and exquisitely wrong, that its substance must be thus reversed in our minds before we can deal with any existing problem of national distress. "To understand that the dispensers of the poor-rates are the almoners of the nation, and should distribute its alms with a gentleness and freedom of hand as much greater and franker than that possible to individual charity, as the collective national wisdom and power may be supposed greater than those of any single person, is the foundation of all law respecting pauperism. " (Since this was written the 'Pall Mall

Gazette' has become a mere party paper—like the rest; but it writes well, and does more good than mischief on the whole.)

{22} [Greek text which cannot be reproduced]

{23} I ought, in order to make this assertion fully understood, to have noted the various weaknesses which lower the ideal of other great characters of men in the Waverley novels—the selfishness and narrowness of thought in Redgauntlet, the weak religious enthusiasm in Edward Glendinning, and the like; and I ought to have noticed that there are several quite perfect characters sketched sometimes in the backgrounds; three—let us accept joyously this courtesy to England and her soldiers—are English officers: Colonel Gardiner, Colonel Talbot, and Colonel Mannering.

{24} Coventry Patmore. You cannot read him too often or too carefully; as far as I know he is the only living poet who always strengthens and purifies; the others sometimes darken, and nearly always depress and discourage, the imagination they deeply seize.

{25} Observe, it is "Nature" who is speaking throughout, and who says, "while she and I together live. "

{26} "Joan of Arc: in reference to M. Michelet's 'History of France. '" De Quincey's Works. Vol. iii. p. 217.

{27} I wish there were a true order of chivalry instituted for our English youth of certain ranks, in which both boy and girl should receive, at a given age, their knighthood and ladyhood by true title; attainable only by certain probation and trial both of character and accomplishment; and to be forfeited, on conviction, by their peers, of any dishonourable act. Such an institution would be entirely, and with all noble results, possible, in a nation which loved honour. That it would not be possible among us, is not to the discredit of the scheme.

{28} See note {19}

{29} That no reference should be made to religious questions.

{30} I have sometimes been asked what this means. I intended it to set forth the wisdom of men in war contending for kingdoms, and what follows to set forth their wisdom in peace, contending for wealth.

{31} See "The Two Paths, " —paragraph beginning "You know I said of that great and pure... "

Copyright © 2021 Esprios Digital Publishing. All Rights Reserved.